The Ugly Truth

My Love Life Sucks!

ESTHER E. LAURENCEAU

PAGE PUBLISHING
Conneaut Lake, PA

First originally published by Page Publishing 2024

ISBN 979-8-88960-290-3 (pbk)
ISBN 979-8-88960-300-9 (digital)

Printed in the United States of America

Contents

Acknowledgments v

About Me..vii

Introduction...ix

Chapter 1:   Lovebug 1

Chapter 2:   Married Man...11

Chapter 3:   The Ideal Boyfriend 16

Chapter 4:   Womanizer..23

Chapter 5:   Blood 33

Chapter 6:   Ghost 39

Chapter 7:   Cop Caller 47

Chapter 8:   Where Are They Now? 72

Acknowledgments

First and foremost, I want to thank my Lord and Savior, Jesus Christ, for loving me unconditionally even at my worst. Hence, for never turning his back on me even though I made plenty of bad choices his love never fails. This unconditional love is nowhere close to the so-called love you get from people. It is unmatched, pure, and comes from a genuine place.

I want to thank my go-getter beloved brother Harry Laurenceau, the second child out of three, for always working hard and making shit happen. I love you and miss you so much! Now that you are gone, life has gotten harder for me. You were right about feeling sorry for me as stated in your letter before you died. It was like you knew I was going to suffer and did not even warn me. Thank you for being the best brother a sister can ask for. Brother, I still cannot believe you are gone. It hurts so much. May you continue to watch over me daily and just know my life sucks without you!

I want to thank my loving mother who is my best friend and my headache. Thank you for instilling morals, values, and work ethics in me. You taught me how to not be lazy and work hard for what I want so that I do not beg anyone for help. You taught me how to pray and have a relationship with God. Thank you. Mommy, I do not always agree with what you do, especially when it comes to your husband; however, it does not disqualify you from being my queen. I love you!

To one of my favorite humble man in the world whom I have the pleasure of knowing and who is one of the best bishops in Brooklyn! Can I get a drum roll please—Bishop Curt E. Courtenay! Thank you for accepting me with open arms in the house of the Lord. Thank you for not judging me. Thank you for your patience and understanding. Thank you for helping me heal in my darkest times. Thank you for demonstrating what leadership really is about and how to be humble in the midst of chaos. I love you so much! I thank God for using you to spread the gospel and help millions. You rock, Bishop!

Thank you, Tony Gaskin, Stephan Labossiere, Ace Metaphor, Steve Harvey, Steven Furlick, Dame Dash, Jennifer Lewis, Sarah Jakes Roberts, Issa Rae, Yvonne Anuli Orji, and Gabrielle Union. You all are truly inspiring and have helped me to get out of my comfort zone.

To those who never met me and only heard gossip about me from others whom I no longer speak to, you all can kiss my soft caramel zebra pillow ass! Now, look at you, reading my book today. Cheers, bitches!

To all the beautiful queens out there, thank you for not giving up! I know it is difficult dealing with a breakup or anything that has not worked out in your favor. Just know that God is always present and will never give you more than you can bear. God will never give up on you, so you might as well stick it out.

PS: Do not give up! Keep on fighting for the life you want, and make sure to consult with God regularly. You got this, sis!

About Me

I always dreamed of getting married one day and being the mother of five handsome boys. I guess God had other plans for me or my selection of men sucks! Whatever it is, my ass is still not in a relationship.

What's good! My name is Esther E. Laurenceau. I am the middle child of three and the only girl. I was born and raised in Kings County Hospital, also known as Killer County. I was the only one who gave my mother a C-section, and to this day, she complains about how much pain I cost her and will sometimes show me her scar. All I could say was damn, I had a big-ass head and weighed a lot!

Thank God I grew up with both of my parents in one household yet only one parent raised me. My mother is more of a sweetheart, and my father is an asshole.

I am a high school and college graduate. I attended Brooklyn Comprehensive Night School and one of the best schools Metropolitan College of New York from August 2016 to June 2019 and obtained my bachelor's degree in human services and was the first in my intermediate to earn that degree. Shout-outs to me! I was fortunate to be taught by high-league professionals who are compassionate and care for the students. Since the age of fourteen, I have worked multiple jobs. My ultimate goal is to become an entrepreneur and be my own boss, make my own rules, and create a schedule that gives me the freedom to live life to the fullest. I do not want to spend my entire life being an employee working for someone else and making their dreams come true and adding more money into his/her pockets. I want to be in control and do what I want in a productive way while making money and living my life. You only get one life. There are no second chances in life, so why not make the best of it? I do not want to die old, bitter, and with regrets. I want to die old, looking young, and at peace.

Introduction

I do not remember the exact date, month, year, or time. But I do remember chilling with one of my cousins in his room who also lived with me at the time. We were talking our shit as per usual, and "he" said, "Yo, E, your love life is like a movie. You stay in some shit and giggle."

One day, I was chilling alone in my room, smoking a blunt, and my mind could not help to think about what my cousin said. I must admit, he was right. Perhaps, I should write a book about my life, then a movie after. That shit would be dope because I am dope. Besides, I am tired of throwing a pity party for myself. It does not change the guys I have dated, and it damn sure will not change the events that took place.

There is a woman or a young girl who needs to hear my story. I am not the first nor will I be the last that has been in a toxic relationship. I want to encourage single women who always attract the wrong men in a relationship that has reached its course and lost their identity.

While you take pleasure in reading my book, do not feel sorry for me (I did enough of that on my own). Take advantage of my advice, and learn from my mistakes. Change starts within, and listening to a preacher's sermon is not enough. You have to have a prayer life. You have to take action. You have to make up your mind to no longer suffer in silence and journal that shit out or do something to express your emotions. Your emotions are powerful, and if you do not know how to control them, they will control you.

Disclaimer: Oh yeah, one more thing before you move into the next chapter. Please make sure the kids are in bed. Do not read this book while they are awake. This book is solely for single women ages fifteen to forty years old. If anyone is below the age limit, please refrain from reading this book. Thank you!

Chapter 1

Lovebug

A girl who does not have a tight-knit relationship with her father will often find herself dating guys with mommy or daddy issues, experiencing trauma, being disrespectful to females in general, being short-tempered, not knowing how to communicate effectively, struggling to commit in a relationship, controlling, jealous, and insecure. You get my point right?

Who does not want to be loved or fall in love? Love is magical. Love is beautiful. Love is a hell of a drug and poisonous if you love the wrong one. According to the Bible, love covers a multitude of sins. Jesus Christ is love. I choose love any day. Shit, I rather love over money.

On a beautiful sunny afternoon, Aries and Cassie were taking a stroll four blocks away from their school and walked past a basketball court full of testosterone. Aries could not help to notice this fine-ass guy who appeared much older than her wearing a white wife beater, black-and-red shorts, and a black durag over his peanut head. She wanted to devour his caramel ass since that shit was sweet anyway. Immediately, Aries told Cassie to take down his number on her behalf; besides, she did not want to appear desperate. At first, Cassie had no problems doing it but later on had some concerns. She did not like the idea of him being older than Aries, being too attractive (which gave him player vibes), and playing basketball in the afternoon rather than doing something productive. Aries truly appreciated Cassie for having her best interest at heart, but this was her choice. Besides, playing basketball is productive as fuck; it is better than smoking weed all day and not doing nothing with your life.

When she first met Race, she was not a virgin at the time. The guy who took Aries's virginity had a little dick and did not know how to use it correctly in the bedroom. To make matters worse, he was a player, and she truly believed his looks saved him, and that is why he had no problems getting girls. Meanwhile, Race and Aries wasted no time making it official and fucking the hell out of each other weekly. The sex was mind-blowing—the best sex she has ever experienced! Although he was her second partner, she could not help to wonder if he was her soul mate. Yup, great sex will have you thinking "he is the one." Aries thought to herself and giggled. Race came with the full package yet lacked *nothing*. He made Aries feel so comfortable in her skin. He taught her a variety of sexual positions, and she enjoyed each of them. He never missed a spot and always made her cum constantly. She regretted that he was not the one to pop her cherry. Can you imagine if he did, her ass would have probably gotten pregnant, and she would have kept the baby too.

Him being a few years older than Aries did not affect their relationship at all. Aries likes dating older guys anyway. She never liked the idea of dating someone younger than her; she likes them old and mature. He was extremely confident, charming, sexy, and popular in his hood. Oftentimes, girls would throw themselves at him, and it did not bother Aries as long he was not entertaining them. They spend a lot of time with each other. They went on dates, worked at the same job thanks to Aries, and attended church together. Overall, they had a Bonnie-and-Clyde relationship.

Mars was laid-back and the person to share your problems with. He never took sides like most people did and heard each party out. He was so understanding and not judging. He always gave humor advice and looked out for others in need. He was the oldest out from all of us. He was neither a charmer nor had luck with the ladies the way his younger siblings did and Race. It sure made sense why Race chose him to be his best friend. He was real.

Race gave Aries the heads-up about a female friend coming over. Aries did not like the idea of his friend coming over but will play cool as long as he behaved himself. Ladies, when your boyfriend has a prep talk with you about any of his female friends coming over, he is only telling you this to make you comfortable and not get out of character. Please be mindful it is all part of his tactics to execute his agenda while he has you thinking they are "just friends." Yeah, aight, keep reading.

The couple sat on the same couch and Lisa sat on a separate couch. Every so often, Aries would observe Race to see if he was staring at Lisa. At first, he did not; but as time went by, he eventually did. Aries thought to herself whatever plans he had in mind, he could kiss that shit goodbye because nothing was going to go down while Aries was alive.

"So what's up, Lisa?" Race asked.

"Nothing much, just chillaxing," Lisa replied.

"It has been a minute since we last saw each other. We talk on the phone a lot but barely see each other," Race said.

Aries charmed in and said, "Oh really."

"And then proceeded and told Race sarcastically you two talk on the phone a lot."

Aries went on and asked Race why he never mentioned anything about him and Lisa talking on the phone.

"Um…" And Race laughed.

Aries was not pleased with his response, and she was ready for his friend to leave. Race offered Lisa something to drink, and she accepted. Race and Lisa remained talking, while Aries stared at Lisa and sucked her teeth. What Aries really wanted to do was grab her by the hair. Race could smell the tension in the room and asked Aries to step out of the living room so they could talk.

"Why are you being so mean to Lisa?"

"She did not do anything wrong," Race said.

"This nigga," Aries mumbled to herself.

"Why were you talking to this bitch?"

"You mention how you have not seen her in a minute. What the fuck is a minute?"

"Are you fucking her?" Aries asked.

"No."

"Yo, you are crazy."

"Just, chill out," Race said.

"Do not tell me what to do!" Aries shouted.

Upon their return to the living room, Aries can tell Lisa was beginning to get uncomfortable and got up to exit. Race followed her to the door, and so did Aries.

If a man lies or cheats on you more than once, he does not respect or give a fuck about you. Stop listening to people who say a guy who lies to a woman is the one he really loves. That is a bald-faced lie and bullshit! If you have to lie to avoid losing your girl, you are going to lose her anyway because she is going to get tired and see you for the scumbag you really are. Once she understands her worth, she has won, and you have lost. As a result, get advice from people who experience the same thing like you, not people who just want to hear you vent and cannot help you. It is a waste of time.

The next female friend was Nia. She was cool and lived around the corner from Mars.

She came over a couple of times to smoke, drink, and talk shit. Aries and Nia hit it off lovely and hung out a few times outside of Mars's parents' house. On one occasion, Aries, Race, Mars, and Jay (who was talking to Nia at the time) were chilling and smoking on the porch. Aries noticed her boyfriend checking out Nia, and she was a little confused as to why he was doing that while his boy was there. She thought to herself maybe it was the weed or this nigga did not care or did not learn his lesson from last time.

Two days later, Aries went over to Mars's parents' house. Race and Mars's younger brother Clad were there smoking. Aries asked Race to step into another room so they could talk.

"What is going on between you and Nia?"

"Are you fucking her?" Aries asked.

"Naw," Race replied.

"She is Jay's girl, and he is the homie," Race added.

"Well, it looks like you two got something going on," Aries said.

"You forgot we were all smoking and motherfuckers were high as shit," Race responded nonchalantly.

"Jay was high, and so was me, but you did not see us gazing into each other's eyes," Aries said.

"If you do not tell me, Nia will," Aries blurted.

"Why you always think I am fucking somebody?" Race asked.

"You do know I have a lot of female friends, right?" Race exclaimed.

Aries walked away.

A few days after they last chilled, Aries saw Nia walking down the block and yelled out her name.

"Nia!"

"Wait up."

"Hey, girl. How is your day going?" Nia asked.

"Girl, chilling," Aries said.

Aries continued to stop beating around the bush and got straight to the point and asked Nia what is up with her.

"Is there something going on between you and Race?"

"No," Nia responded.

"What made you say that?" Nia asked.

"The day we were all chilling on the stoop, I watched you two undress each other with your eyes."

Nia laughed.

"What!" Nia shouted.

"Girl, you are tripping. We are just friends," Nia said.

"If I did that to Jay, you would have felt some type of way, am I right or wrong?" Aries asked.

"No, I would not," Nia responded.

"Okay," Aries said.

The two went in opposite directions. Before crossing the street, Aries took one last glance at Nia.

Mars's girlfriend, Gin, and Aries went to the same school. In fact, they had a few mutual friends in common but never said a word to one another. Gin was not the best-looking thing in town, but she did have a body, though no homo. Mars was ugly; however, it did not change the fact that he was a good, faithful dude, which is a plus if you ask me. It was so rare to find faithful men then and even harder today. So, ladies, if you ever come across one, treat him right. Do not,

I repeat, look to see if the grass is greener on the other side. You will regret it. You better work with the grass you got now; it will grow eventually if it is meant.

Gin was cool, down to earth, very popular, and hit it off fine with the fellas easily. Aries admired girls like Gin—not too many female friends and hung around boys more. It made perfect sense why they got along. Without a doubt, their friendship moved pretty quickly, and it turned into something meaningful. In Aries's eyes, Gin was no longer considered a friend; she was more like the sister she never had. Almost every day after school, they hung out at Gin's mother's house, who happened to be a dope person as well. Ms. Jefferson was a force to not reckon with; she had no filter, was down to earth, energetic, and a mother figure to anybody who crossed paths with her. To add on, Ms. Jefferson knew how to throw it down in the kitchen!

One summer afternoon, Aries, Race, Mars, and Gin chilled in a parking lot of a beach smoking, drinking, listening to music, and cracking jokes before getting out of the jeep to go for a swim. From time to time, Race would check on Aries and offer her to join him in the water. She let her foot rest in the water, then ran away when the wave got closer to her.

Things between Mars and Gin were moving pretty fast, and he fell in love with her instantly whereas Gin did not feel the same way. Gin wanted to take things slow. Carlos, who lived down the block from Gin, were close friends. He was cool, had a huge sense of humor, was bisexual, Christian, and energetic. Jayden, on the other hand, to Aries's surprise, was dating Gin.

"Oh shit," Aries exclaimed.

"What the fuck?" Aries said.

This chick was bold, Aries thought to herself.

She was really feeling this dude and illustrated more affection than she did with Mars. She might as well whoop out his dick and start fucking him in front of us. Jayden was definitely an upgrade from Mars. He was dark-skinned, handsome, had a nice physique and long coolie hair, and definitely gave Aries player vibes.

Meanwhile, Race was still bringing bitches to Mars's parents' house and got comfortable talking to any chick who caught his attention outside. He showed no remorse, and Aries could not take it anymore yet had a hard time breaking up with him. This was her first serious relationship ever and the love of her life. She was not interested in no one else except Race. He knew that and still could not keep his dick in his pants. They constantly argue, go months or days without speaking to each other, then reappear in each other's lives again. It was toxic, but that dick and tongue game was irresistible!

Here we go, his ass strikes again! This motherfucker will never learn. It was the ultimate betrayal from both parties. Aries did not know who to address first; she was baffled as to the person she called a sister and chilled with daily to do some fuckery like this. Out of all the guys who were lusting after her, she had to go fuck my nigga. Goddamn! Ain't that a bitch. Aries needed answers and reached out to Race first. Surprisingly, he did not deny anything and told her the truth from the beginning to the end, and that was the last time Race heard from Aries. Aries contacted Gin next, and this trifling bitch did not answer her phone. She even pulled up to her momma's house, and no one answered the door. She waited a while before leaving to inquire the neighbors about Gin's whereabouts, and a few of them said they had not seen her lately. Aries continues with her search and looks for Gin's nasty-ass in school and all their mutual friends claim they have not heard from or seen her. One thing for sure the bitch could not hide for long: Aries will find her ass sooner or later. This is not over!

Ever since Race came clean with Aries about his so-called female friends, she could not take him seriously after that or even be in the same room with him. She felt disgusted, and she knew damn well this nigga was not wearing any protection. Not that it will change anything if he did because he lied to her face. They did not officially call it quits but lost communication for a while. Unfortunately, that was not the only problem Aries was stressing over; she was mourning over the loss of her brother, the one she grew up with and was close to. It took that one loss to make Aries forget about everything and move to Georgia.

Living in Georgia was dry as fuck! It was nothing like New York. Everything was so damn far to get around. Also, Aries was not the type to ask others for a ride. She would rather not go out than depend on others to get by. She knew this stay would be temporary. There was no way she could live in those conditions.

As for her cousins, she was very grateful for them and admired her godmother even more for letting her live with her family at such short notice. She just could not live in New York knowing it would make things worse for her now that her brother was no longer alive. As for her eldest brother, he lived miles away from her. There was no way Aries could just visit him whenever she wanted to. Where he resided was too far, and nothing but violence surfaced around. Aries did not understand how her brother Nick put up with his living situation. It was not like he had no choice; he had a choice and decided to remain where he was at. It was annoying. Anyway, you cannot tell a grown-ass person what to do. People are going to do what the fuck they want no matter how much you beg them not to. She still loves him, though!

The curriculum in Georgia was much harder than New York. Aries could not keep up. High school felt more like college; everything was fast-paced, and you barely got one-to-one with the teachers. So she spent most of her time in house detention eating one of the best chicken sandwiches and writing what she did wrong hundred times and cracking jokes with one of her cousins toward the teacher. Yes! The math class sucked. Aries hated Math ever since she was introduced to it. Whoever created Math must have lived a boring ass life, did not get any pussy, and a fucking lame. But the motherfucker was smart because math is needed everywhere.

There were a few cuties that caught Aries's attention, but she did not take them seriously. The guys in Georgia are way different than the guys in New York. Men from New York have natural swags, unlike Georgia men who do not and try too hard. That is just my opinion. Aries was not impressed by that. She definitely became popular in the neighborhood thanks to her wonderful cousins and also stood out from the rest since she was from New York. As time went by, that was how they addressed her as —New York. It was cool.

"Hey, how is it going?" Aries asked.

"Do you know who this is?" Aries continue.

"Hell yeah, I do," Race replied.

"It is my best friend, the love of my life," Race said.

"I miss you a whole lot," Race added.

"Where are you?" Race asked.

Aries mentioned, "She resides in Georgia after her brother died."

"Oh shit," Race replied.

"Your brother died?" Race continued.

"Damn, I am so sorry to hear that," Race mentioned.

"Race, you know you hurt me a lot. Why did you do it?" Aries asked.

"You were my everything and my first relationship. You played the shit out of me."

"I know. I fucked up big-time," Race said.

"I am so sorry, and I never meant to hurt you," Race added.

"I was young and dumb and did not understand how to be in a serious relationship," Race expressed.

"You were the first girl who has ever taken me seriously," Race disclosed.

"I know saying sorry is too late and it will not change anything, but I am deeply sorry," Race said.

"I hear you," Aries responded.

Aries went on and asked Race, "How is life?"

Race informed Aries of him moving to Philadelphia, and how he has a daughter now.

He further went into details and told Aries that he was not with the child's mother and how she was crazy.

Aries laughed and mentioned how her life has not been the same ever since the passing of her brother.

"You are my best friend, my everything. I miss you," Aries expressed.

"Do you have Facebook?" Aries asked.

"No," Race replied.

"Yeah, I reached out to your friends and asked about you prior to me reaching out to you. No one has heard from you," Aries said.

"Yeah, I do not keep tabs with anyone anymore, but I really miss you all," Race added.

"Well, it was nice hearing from you again," Aries said.
"Yeah, me too. I love you, Aries," Race said.
"Love you too, Race. Bye," Aries replied.
"Bye. Save my number." Aries then hanged up the phone.

Chapter 2

Married Man

Take your time, and do not rush when getting to know someone. Sometimes a man will tell you everything you want to hear to make it seem like he is really into you. Maybe you are in a vulnerable space, got out of a bad breakup, or are afraid of being alone. Whatever that is, trust your instinct and move slowly. You do not want to start something fast and it ends fast.

Aries was beautiful, and it was hard for any man not to look when she walked by. Her personality was eccentric, and with that smile of hers, she would light up any room. Men oftentimes hollered at her whether she dressed up or not. Honestly, she did not like that kind of attention and was mesmerized by her beauty anyway.

She attended a medical assistant program in Manhattan for nine months. At the time, she was fed up with her life and wanted to make up for all the lost time wasted in school. Beforehand, Aries thought she had all the time in the world and was not thinking about how her choices could impact her badly in the long run. She was in her early twenties and thought she had all the time in the world to screw up. Her brother's death was an eye-opener for her. Unfortunately, it took something bad to happen to wake her the fuck up and straighten out her life. Her goal was to complete the program: graduate on time, get a job afterward, and refrain from any distractions.

Her being under stress did not keep her from laughing, and she was not going to hold her laugh in than suffocate. Anytime Aries saw or heard something, funny she laughed. There was no way she could ignore people who made her laugh, and from that point on, the rest was memorable. Matthew, Cali, Annie, Meca, and Ava were some dope-ass people she had ever encountered. They had similar and different backgrounds yet had the same common goal, which was graduating and having fun no matter what obstacles came in their direction. They were their own little family. Whenever Aries went through some shit, Cali was whom she confined the most. Cali was good at giving advice even though she had problems of her own.

They went out to eat, club, karaoke, and bowl; and that was one of the best highlights of Aries's life. She was not used to hanging out with positive people and it was different.

One weekend, they all head out for brunch in the city and Matthew brought a plus-one. Overall, Aries likes guys with tattoos, a little aggressive, not too extreme, hood, piercings on both ears, coolie hair, dreadlocks, waves, braids, dark skin, caramel, tall, a little chubby, not fat, big eyes, and packing. Anything not listed above was a hard pass. Man! *He fits the description*, Aries thought to herself. Gangster, hood, caramel, short, a little chubby, not fat, coolie hair, and beautiful round eyes—immediately she was turned on. Although she liked what she saw, she had to play cool for the sake of her peers watching and, most importantly, not appear thirsty.

Out of all the seats, he sat across from Aries. Her classmates could not help to cheer them on except for Matthew, who did not find anything exciting in that. It was cute and embarrassing at the same time. Aries was not used to that. She even noticed Matthew whispering something to the dude; she did not know if it was a warning sign or what. Despite everything happening right before her eyes, Aries could not help to think about Danger and his whereabouts. Danger was someone she met through a mutual friend at the time who also disapproved of them two hooking up since he was a certified player. They were fucking for fun until she later caught feelings. Aries was a sucker for love and liked being in love. Even though things did not last with Race, she still loved him. Danger was cool, laid-back, and always tried to avoid the possibility of dating Aries. Every time she mentioned it, he always found an excuse to justify his reasons for not wanting to be with her. What caught her off guard and brought confusion was the fact that Danger treated Aries like his girl. They did a lot of couple shit together.

She wanted to fuck him that day but did not want to risk losing the opportunity of knowing this fine brother sitting across from her in this nice restaurant with dim lights and artificial decor. This fancy restaurant had good-quality food, and it was inexpensive. They wasted no time exchanging numbers.

"What is your name?" Aries asked.

"Rasheed."

"What is your name?" Rasheed asked.

"Aries."

On their way back home, Aries and Rasheed spoke throughout the ride, and a few of the peers chip in once in a while, but it was clear the attention was on them.

They spoke on the phone frequently and were eager to see one another. On several occasions, he invited her out, but Aries was not working and did not want to rely on him to pay for anything. And she damn sure was not going to use the unemployment money she needed for other important matters.

During her medical assistant training, Rasheed supported her by allowing Aries to practice drawing blood on him and taking his blood pressure. They smoke weed and talk about anything. She could not wait to see what he was working with. The more she cummed, the more he ate her out even when she begged him to stop because that shit drove her crazy. She did not want him to starve, so she cooperated and moaned while he did his thing. His tongue game was amazing! Unfortunately, his penis was small like her pinkie. Look at the bright side, at least he did not lack in other areas in the bedroom, she thought to herself. He sure exceeded her expectations.

It was never official although they spoke about dating. His excuse was he was not looking for anything serious and needed to concentrate on his life, blah, blah, blah. Yet he did not mind fucking the hell out of her on a weekly basis.

"We need to talk," Rasheed blurted out.

"I am listening," Aries replied.

"Do you remember the sex video we made?" Rasheed asked.

"Yeah, why?" Aries said.

"My wife saw it," Rasheed mentioned.

"Excuse me?" Aries asked.

"Your what?" Aries asked again.

"My wife," Rasheed replied.

"Nigga…your what?" Aries said shockingly.

"You heard me. Stop playing," Rasheed responded.

"No, you stop playing," Aries replied angrily.

"Your ass is married?" Aries said with disbelief.

"Why did you wait so long to tell me this?" Aries asked.

"What the fuck is wrong with you?" Aries persisted.

Rasheed paused for a few seconds before responding. "I do not know."

"Were you two together when we first met?" Aries asked.

"No. She was locked up," Rasheed replied.

"Wow," Aries replied.

"Your ass was trying to get me killed," Aries said shockingly.

Rasheed laughed.

"That shit is not funny. I am being serious," Aries said.

"Do you have kids with her?" Aries elaborated on the subject a little more further.

"Yes. Two from her and one from my other baby mother, but we are not together, and she barely let me see my son," Rasheed replied.

"What the fuck!" Aries shouted.

"How many baby mothers do you have?" Aries asked.

"Two," Rasheed responded.

"What else are you lying about?" Aries exclaimed.

"My age," Rasheed said.

"What!" Aries shouted.

"How old are you, asshole?" Aries asked.

"Nineteen," Rasheed replied.

"Okay, this is too much. You need to get the fuck out of my crib," Aries shouted.

"Yo, chill. Let us talk about this. I am sorry."

"If I told you this from the beginning, you would have never given me a chance," Rasheed mentioned.

"I really like you," Rasheed continued.

"Yo, get the fuck out. I don't want to see or speak to you again. Fuck off!" Aries slammed the door. Aries knew this was a dead-end situation. She did not like being in this position and would not want the same thing to happen to her when she gets married. Plus, being a side piece was not an option if she was not the main chick. *Fuck out of here. This nigga got me fuck up!*

Chapter 3

The Ideal Boyfriend

Everyone desires to meet the love of their life—someone to come home to or begin a family with. Of course, Aries is not belittling any woman who is single. She perfectly understands why some women are single and that is okay. She is only referring to herself. Being single can be boring, especially during the holidays, cold winter months, and rainy days.

Today is a big day! Aries's long-time friend Sheri from elementary school was pregnant and invited her to her baby shower. It had been a while since they hung out, so attending the baby shower early would give them enough time to catch up. Sheri was glowing and looked so adorable in her fitted olive-green silk dress. When it came to fashion, this girl was on point from head to toe. Aries never saw her mismatched any of her clothes and always color coordinated. Whenever Aries was on her period, she preferred to stay home or wear all black or dark colors when going out. Aries has a thing where she always checked to see if her pad needed to be changed or intact. On her way back from the restroom, while coming down the stairs, she noticed this gorgeous, handsome man looking at her. He was dark-skinned, had a low caesar with waves spinning for days, and even smiled and winked at her. She smiled back and blush but did not wink back. He would have laughed if she did. She sucked at winking. He was so fine and looked delicious. Aries could not help but reflect on that soft dark Hershey skin of his; it was breathtaking!

Hours into the baby shower, the host called out for everyone to come together to play a game, and this was an opportunity for Aries to go for the kill. Instead, she visualized herself making out with him. During the game, they both yelled out things while sitting across from each other, and she ended up stopping to not make it look obvious.

"Congratulations, boo!" Aries shouted.

"Thank you for the invite," Aries continued.

"Girl, you are very welcome. It was good seeing you, long-time friend," Sheri stated.

"Same here," Aries replied.

"Hey, do you know anyone who can give me a ride home?" Aries asked.

Aries could have easily called her pops to come pick her up, but she chose not to.

Sheri wasted no time smiling and asked the cutie to take her home. Guess what? He did not decline either. Aries thought it would be them two in the car; however, it turned out to be multiple people whom she knew. Apparently, the people he was dropping off were Aries's mother's church friends. *What the hell?* Aries thought it was funny and humiliating at the same time, hoping this ride ends on a good note. You just never know with Haitian parents and what comes out of their mouths. They have no shame in their game. Hopefully, they do not fuck up her ride by interrogating her.

This guy had a sense of humor, which was a plus for Aries. She was a natural fool at heart and was raised in a family with huge sense of humors. Although her family was not perfect and had issues, she was grateful for the humor. It was something she would cherish forever even if everyone parts ways, which eventually happened since her family was divided anyway. Nothing has been the same since her brother died. He definitely caught Aries by surprise when he spoke Creole; she did not know he was Haitian. Minutes after dropping the remaining two, it was only Aries left. He could have easily dropped her home first, yet he was smart enough to drop her last. His ass thought he was slick, and it got her excited.

"What is your name by the way?" Aries asked.

"Jaheim."

"Yours?"

"Aries."

There is no way she was going to let Jahiem slide into another female vagina and not hers first! He looked good. Jaheim had an average dick—not too big and not too small. His tongue game was good. The problem was him nutting too fast. What the fuck, yo? It annoyed the crap out of her a lot. He must have had a health condition or something. It did not make sense. She felt cheated. She was not done, nor did she cum. It was a slap to her face. Unbelievable.

One time, when they finished being intimate, they lay there and smoked.

"Why do you nut so fast?" Aries inquired.

"You do not give me a chance to cum that is selfish!" Aries exclaimed.

"The pussy feels so good, and I cannot hold my nut if it is ready to come out." Jahiem laughed.

"Damn, that is crazy," Aries said.

Aside from that, Jahiem never had an issue spending time with her. They went to church together. He dropped and picked her up from school, and they ate and smoked weed together. He spent the holidays with her and her family who admired and treated Jahiem like a son-in-law already. It was so cute, and Aries felt complete at that moment. She really believed this was the man she would spend the rest of her life with and have children by. Speaking of children, they did try plenty of times, and it was unsuccessful.

Aries's parents, especially her father, are very judgmental and never approve of any man she brings around. At the end of the day, Aries did not care about their opinions; it was her life and her choices. She was no longer a child and an adult, which her parents failed to realize and accept. Let me school you real quick: Any Haitian child can attest to this. It does not matter how old you are as long as you are living in a Haitian household. Be prepared to be treated like a kid until you move out and get your own apartment. Until then, it is the parent's roof and their rules.

Jahiem was the first guy that her parents actually got along with. They welcomed him with open arms and showed him lots of love, whether it was her mom making his favorite ice tea, which he loved so much, or her pops coming out with his toolbox to fix any malfunction in his car or her cousins comparing him to Brian McKnight, chilling and drinking with him. It was all love. Jahiem was definitely that guy, and his personality was contagious. He was cool and fun to be around. Aries truly admired the person that he was.

No one is perfect; no relationship is perfect. Sometimes you have to know what is worth fighting for or worth letting go. Jahiem had another lifestyle that he disliked discussing with Aries. She understood that they move much quicker than expected, but it did not make it excusable to keep certain things from her. She needed to know who the fuck he really was. God forbid someone was after him. She would know how to move accordingly.

Never keep secrets from your significant other, especially when you are living a double life or have a dark past. The other person deserves to know what is going on. Your actions do not affect the person you are dating only; it also affects those who are associated with that person. If you do not trust someone with your deepest secrets, then why are you with that person?

"Who got you cheesing like that over the phone?" Cindy asked.

"My boyfriend, Jahiem," Aries replied. Aries was a private person and did not share her love life with just anybody only a few people knew.

"What are your intentions with my cousin?" Kimberly asked.

"We are dating," Jahiem responded.

Jahiem remained quiet afterward. "I will call you later on, babe. I got to go."

"Okay," Aries replied.

Automatically, Aries assumed he was either cheating or did not want to be with her anymore. He never called back. She went weeks without hearing from him, and she was beginning to get worried.

One night, Aries got a call from an unknown number. Usually, she never responded to numbers not saved in her contact list and it went to voice mail. However, something told her to answer and it was a male voice. The male voice was talking to Aries like he knew her for years, which made her comfortable even though she had no clue who it was. Besides, she was bored anyway. The guy would not reveal his real name but instead told Aries his street name, which was Shark.

"Are you dating anyone?" Shark asked.

"Yes, and why do you want to know?" Aries inquired.

"Just asking," Shark replied.

Even though she told him yes, it did not stop him from trying to flirt with her. From that point on, she sensed something was not right about this picture. Yes, he was funny as hell and made her laugh, but it was not like she was going to hook up with nigga. They were on the phone for a while, talking about random shit.

"Do you have any single friends?"

Aries responded yes before hanging up the phone. Aries did not trust him.

A few minutes after they hung up, Aries's phone rang again, and this time she was not going to answer in case it was Shark's annoying ass. He seemed cool over the phone but someone she would not become friends with. She did not trust him. Since she was bored, she decided to answer once again, and guess who it was: Jahiem. The audacity to disappear, not return her calls, and think the shit was acceptable. To top it off, this nigga got the balls to start wilding out and being disrespectful without acknowledging her or giving an explanation about his whereabouts.

"What the fuck is your problem?" Jahiem asked.

"I go out of town, and you are already interested in fucking other guys," Jahiem said angrily.

"What are you talking about? You sound stupid," Aries responded.

"Lower your fucking voice when you talking to me. Who the fuck you think you are?" Aries exclaimed.

"If anything, I should be the one who is furious, not you," Aries said.

"You go ghost on me, and now you want to be disrespectful?" Aries implied.

"Did you enjoy that last conversation?" Jahiem asked nonchalant.

"Is that how you move when I am not around?" Jahiem continued.

"Oh shit!" Aries whispered.

"You set me up. How did I not catch sight of that?" Aries said.

"Wow, you are very childish." Jahiem was so upset and hung up the phone.

Aries contacted him back numerous times, and he never answered. She even texted him, and he ignored her. She even reached out to Shark's trifling ass, and he claimed he had not heard from him but could hear Jahiem cursing and talking crap in the background.

"Put him on the phone," Aries told Shark.

"He does not want to speak to you," Shark replied.

"It is your fault. Why would you agree to prank me like this? You are fucked up," Aries said angrily.

Shark laughed.

"Yo, hang up the phone on her," Jahiem shouted in the background.

"No, wait," Aries said.

"Shark, hang up the phone."

Aries was so pissed and angry that this shit was happening to her all over again. The games that these men—she meant boys—played were out of control. They just did not care.

"You have a collect call from Jahiem."

"Hello. What happened to you?" Aries asked.

"I have been calling you nonstop, and you never return my calls," Aries went on.

Jahiem informed Aries he was in jail."

"What?" Aries asked.

"For what?" Aries asked again.

"They pick me up at the gas station in Florida," Jahiem said.

"For what?" Aries responded.

There was a pause. "Drugs," Jahiem stated.

"Oh wow," Aries replied.

"How long are you going to be there?" Aries asked. Jahiem said he does not know.

"Wow, you need to tell me everything that happened," Aries told Jahiem.

"I will when I come home. I do not want to talk about that now," Jahiem replied.

"Meanwhile, can you do me a favor and send me money on my books?" Jahiem asked.

"I am also going to write to you too," Jahiem added.

"Okay, I got you," Aries responded.

"Damn, I am going to miss you a lot," Aries added.

"Me too. I love you," Jahiem said.

"I love you too," Aries responded.

The phone hung up.

When a guy gets locked up, he makes all the promises in the world and pretends that he has changed and will treat you better. He is the sweetest when behind bars. But the moment he comes home, physics on point, that is when his ego kicks in and he forgets about the girl who has always held him down to chase after bitches who would never do half of the things that the main girlfriend did.

They wrote to each other constantly. She even sent money to his books and gave him anything he needed.

Chapter 4

Womanizer

Aries got tired of dealing with the same type of men and getting nowhere. Love should not be this hard to find. It was so easy to have sex than to find her person. She did not want to go on like this, and it was beginning to feel as if she was not meant to be loved after all. She got tired of rooting for other people in love; meanwhile, no one was rooting for her. She felt like shit. At times, she felt like God was purposely punishing her, yet she did not blame God. She was hard-headed and often did her own thing without taking it into prayer. She wanted to be a wife and have children someday. She did not want to be the long-time girlfriend anymore, the experimental girlfriend, or the woman who ends up in situationships. She was tired of selling herself short and wanted something real which was challenging to find within this generation.

Whenever she was on social media and came across pictures of couples, she sort of envied them. They made it seem like love was so easy to find and that was not her reality. Her dating world was consumed with lust, taken advantage of, lied to, cheated on, verbally abused, physically abused, and getting arrested—one of the worst betrayals among the rest.

She wanted to attract something different than what she normally attracts. Sometimes she watched herself in the mirror and just stood there, wondering what men saw in her that she did not see in herself. What was it that drew them to her? Whatever it was, Aries was running out of patience and time and needed guidance in this area. Her choice of men was awful, and sometimes it made her feel awful. She wondered if pussy and her looks were all that she had to offer. She did not want to grow old and single or be successful and single. She still wanted to hold on to her independence like the bad bitch she was but also wanted to experience true love with someone. No money or success can truly fill in that void but God anyway. That is why you see a lot of celebrities overdose or commit suicide because money is not enough to make them happy, and neither is someone else. Money is just a temporary, quick fix, but God's love and peace are eternal.

When Aries saw this man, immediately she was turned off by him. The dude was ugly. She took a quick glance at his friends and still did not give him a chance. She was fed up and wanted something real and long-term nothing less. Laura goofy ass decided to introduce Aries and the guy who was staring at her during the middle of service. Laura could not wait until service was over. Why was she feening? Aries laughed at her and told Laura that she was not interested and got up to go to the restroom. Laura watched her walk away. Upon her return, she noticed the guy sitting behind her seat. Laura was Aries's childhood friend and even had the same babysitter. Prior to the service, they had not seen each other in a long time, and now they were catching up.

While Laura and Aries were going back and forth, he complimented her hair, and she thanked him without a smile so he did not get any idea that he has a shot with her. Besides, Aries was not completely over Rasheed and Jahiem yet.

One day, Aries went to one of her friends' baby showers at her church, and guess who happened to be there—the same guy. Aries was beginning to think this guy had a tracking device attached to her car or something. She did not quite understand why she kept on running into him. It did not matter if they had mutual friends or not. However, she kept her word and refused to give in. Next thing you know, this guy had the audacity to sit right next to her. She was annoyed and observed his friends watching from afar like they just finished making a bet with him to see if he would get her number. Another thing that threw Aries off about this was the fact that one of the girls appeared twice his age out of the rest of his friends, who were much younger. That was weird but whatever.

One thing about Aries is when she is not interested in someone, no one can force or change her mind. Every time he sat closer to her, she moved away from him, and his friends would laugh and make fun of his goofy ass. He did not even care how he appeared to friends; he was on a mission. He was persistent and would not take no for an answer. Aries not going to front his efforts of winning her over was intriguing to watch, but her answer still remained the same: no.

In the long run, Aries realizes men pretend very well in the beginning, especially if they are chasing after pussy. They are going to say all the right things you want to hear at the right time and use it to their advantage, and if you are in a vulnerable stage, it is a wrap! Your mind will have you thinking you found your match made from heaven, and toward the end, it turns out to be a fucking lie.

Aries was at a church function when she saw this man for the third time in the same year. It was becoming too much, and she was convinced he was a stalker. He sat right beside her.

"Are you enjoying the service?" the man asked.

"Yes," Aries replied.

"How often do you read the Bible?" the man inquired.

"Sometimes," Aries responded.

Although she was curious to know why they kept running into each other and wanted to ask him if he was following her, she did not let it bother her and continued with the service. As soon as service ended, he wasted no time and walked Aries to her room, and they stood in the lobby chatting.

"My name is Jason."

"What is your name?"

"Aries."

In the middle of their conversation, a girl who knew Jason ran off out of nowhere, and his dumb ass decided to join her. Aries was a bit startled by the whole thing and was trying to figure out if God was warning her about him or if she should exit.

A couple of minutes later, he returned and apologized, then they exchange numbers. Just so you know, this was not the end of the conversation, and it would be brought up once Aries cooled off and process what just happened.

Jason was not someone she normally went for, and Aries decided to give him a chance anyway despite the red flags God allowed her to see in the early stage. Ladies, when God allows you to see someone for who they really are, believe him. Do not ever—I repeat, do not ever—look back! Do not become curious. You do not have to know everything; the less you know, the better for you to heal. Learn to love yourself, and know when to walk away. And when God reveals those red flags in the early stage, believe and listen to God because he knows every person's true intentions, and all he is trying to do is protect you from getting your feelings hurt. If you do not listen to God, you will be very disappointed in the long run, and it will be too late. The damage is already done.

She thought trying something different would bring different results, but what she learned over time was if her approach is the same, she would not see different results.

They spoke on the phone every day. Aries wanted to move at a slower pace, and so did he, which was a plus. She knew inviting him over would not be an issue since he was a "church boy," and her parents admired that, especially her mom since she was a devoted Christian. Let me set the record straight, though: Just because someone goes to church does not mean one has a relationship with God. Anybody can believe in God, anybody can call themselves a Christian, and anybody can go to church; and it means absolutely nothing. There is nothing wrong with her mom favoring such men, but she needs to be mindful and not be deceived because there are men who have a better relationship with God and never attended church than those who does regularly.

They finally had some one-on-one time after talking on the phone for months. This would be the first time they actually hung out. They did not know where to hang out, so instead of roaming in the street, he thought it would be a good idea to chill at the park, but Aries declined and told him they could just chill right here outside in her neighborhood just to play safe on her end in case he was a psychopath. They spoke briefly, and he kept gazing into her eyes. From the looks of things, you can tell he wanted to devour her tongue. Aries not going to the front she was kind of skeptical observing his ugliness. *What if he does not know how to kiss? What if we get caught by someone we know?* They already had enough mutual friends, and she will be damned for this shit to be brought up in the pastor's sermon on Sunday.

At first, Aries was playing hard to get, and he got closer to her. So she gave him a peck just to tease him a little and yes it felt good. Afterward, they both went in, and all she could say was damn, she hit the jackpot! At that point, she did not want to stop. She said to herself that if they were not outside, she would have ripped his clothes off just to see what he was working with. Yeah, he may be ugly in the face, but that tongue of his was something powerful. Damn…A few weeks after their initial meeting, he invited her over to his place, and it was obvious that he was renting a room. There were cats everywhere, and Aries was not with the shit. She almost tripped over one of the steps running away from them. Thank God, Jason was not there to witness that. Aries told his ass straight up to take the cats upstairs or she was out. He pleaded with her and told her they were harmless and would not be in the way. She still was not convinced and wanted them out of her sight. He brought them upstairs.

They chilled and talked for a bit. Jason even offered Aries to read the Bible while each of them took turns. Aries thought that was cute and all but was also distracted by his physique. For an ugly dude, his body was intact. He had muscles and abs, and Aries wanted a taste of all that sweetness. "Why the hell he wore a wife beater and sweats?" she said to herself. Men who had nice bodies and wore sweats made her weak. He had a nice firm butt too, and it was irresistible. She wanted to grab it and bite it. She never met a guy who took good care of his body besides Jahiem after he got out of prison. His shit was nice too, and Aries enjoyed every muscle of his body. She used to suck on his nipple too. Sorry, you guys! I had a flashback. Back to Jason! She played along and did as instructed then went for the kill again, but he kept on resisting, and she was confused as to why he did not want to have sex with her. She hope this nigga was not gay.

"What is up with you?" Aries asked.

"Why do you not want to have sex with me?" Aries added.

"I just want us to read the Bible," Jason said.

"I want to get to know you better before we have sex," Jason explained.

Aries was not used to any guy telling her this and did not take him seriously. In the back of her mind, she felt as if he was playing hard to get, which turned her on even more. "C'mon, stop playing. You know you want me." He was still resisting.

As time went by, Jason realized that Aries was a force to be reckoned with and would not take no for an answer. Next thing you know, clothes were flying everywhere. Damn, just writing about this is making me wet! He was one of the best dicks I ever had. I am crying! I miss you!

Besides Race and Monk, Jason was a winner! Everything was on point, and he was definitely packing! OMG…OMG. When I die, I want him to be buried on top of me.

His butt—oh, his butt—was so soft and firm. Aries could not take her hands off it. Also, it kept her safe and alive. Do not get her started on the sex; that shit was one of the best things she had ever experienced. The way Jason kissed, ate, and stroked made her feel like she was on cloud nine. She never wanted the sex to end. It was bananas! She could not believe it was actually happening and did not regret it not one bit. Thereafter, when they both cummed, the doorbell rang. Aries was not expecting any company, and she damn sure did not tell anyone about her whereabouts, so who the fuck was ringing his doorbell. She wasted no time getting dressed. Fuck being naked under the covers! When he went to answer the door, she tagged along too. She stood near his bedroom door to not make herself hot and peeked her head out since the door was a few inches away. Yo, it was the same fucking girl who ran off the first time with two other male friends! "Oh hell naw!" Aries said to herself. "This cannot be real. What the fuck?" Aries was livid! Something was definitely going on between them. This bitch was too comfortable with no care in the world. She could have called first, you know. To not make a scene, Aries ran back to his room and closed the door. She was angry.

After hours of being left in his room alone, upon his return, Aries told him she was ready to leave. "Are you two dating?" Aries asked.

"No, we are just friends," Jason said.

"They came over so we can go to rehearsal," Jason added.

"I am the only one who has access to the van," Jason further discussed.

Unfortunately, Aries fell for his lies, and they proceeded to go outside. Aries was very uncomfortable being in the van with all of them. She was a woman herself and knew when two people were more than just friends. Aries and the girl made eye contact from time to time, and then Aries looked at Jason to see his reaction. She even caught him checking out another woman who was jogging and felt disrespected. Aries did not know which one was worse: the chick that ran off in the lobby sitting in this damn van or the other woman minding her business and jogging. Aries was curious into learning more about this girl that ran off. She just could not get this bitch out of her mind. So as the investigator that she was, she went on Facebook to look her up, and the things that she discovered confirmed that Jason was lying all along. That girl was not his friend; they were dating exclusively. Between the mutual friends, they had and the church community they were an item. Another clue was the comments from the pictures and statuses Jason wrote and vice versa. At that point, the trust was gone, but the sex kept Aries coming back.

To make matters worse, after she discovered this girl was his girlfriend, there were other girls in the picture. Yes! Aries does a very good job investigating shit. Since he was not being honest with her, she had to do her own digging. Aries wasted no time airing him out on Facebook. She did not directly tag his name in the status, but he knew it was about him. The phone rang.

"Is everything okay?" Jason asked.

"Yeah, why?" Aries replied.

"No reason. Just checking on you," Jason implied.

"Is that all?" Aries continue.

"Yeah," Jason responded.

The more she discovered things about him, the more he lied to her. Just like he cheated on her, she cheated on him too. The only difference was she never got caught. Even though she cheated on him, she still wanted to be with him and was going to put in the work to make the relationship work. He was the love of her life, her everything, and there was no way she was going to break up with him, especially with that dick of his. That was her dick.

Jason was not the type of guy who likes to communicate; he was that guy who would go to sleep upset. Aries did not like going to sleep mad; she liked to express herself and talk things out. It made her more annoyed that he did not want to talk. Getting him to talk was like pulling teeth. But when he was hollering at girls, chilling with his friends, and watching *The Walking Dead*, he had a lot to say.

Ladies, when someone no longer wants you and just sticks around for the benefits, just leave and never look back. Do not try to work things out unless both parties want to work things out. Learn to love yourself and walk away when someone devalues you. Aries did everything she could to make Jason stop cheating on her. She brought him things, gave him money, and allowed him to move in with her; but the cheating would not end. She thought allowing him to move in with her would strengthen their relationship and bring them closer. It definitely backfired on her. The cheating was happening more frequently in front of her house. He still refused to communicate whenever they had a disagreement. It was bad.

One day, Aries came home from work; and when she walked into her room, she sensed tension and disliked the look on his face.

"What is wrong?" Aries asked.

"We need to talk," Jason said.

"Talk about what?" Aries proceeded to ask.

"I found another spot to live," Jason responded.

"What!" Aries blurted.

"Why?" Aries asked with tears coming down her face.

"I need my own space. I need some time to clear my mind," Jason replied.

"I will give you all the space you need, so you can clear your mind here," Aries expressed.

"No, I have to leave," Jason insisted.

"What is it? Talk to me. Whatever it is, we can figure it out slowly," Aries mentioned.

He got up and watched the tears fall down Aries's face and gave her a napkin. Aries was so hurt; nothing she said changed his mind. He had his bags packed and was ready to leave. He even told Aries he would get the rest of his belongings another day. That was when she saw red and told him no.

"Since you want to walk out, walk out with everything! You are not stepping foot in this house again." And she started throwing his stuff down the stairs. When her father heard all the commotion going on, he quickly intervened and asked Jason what happened. Both of them sat in the living room, talking for hours, while Aries remained upstairs hurt. After their conversation, Aries asked her pops what they talked about.

"He never wanted to be with you, and you begged him to have sex with you," Aries's father stated.

At that point, all bets were off. This nigga violated her and disrespected her pops. Like why the fuck would he disclose those details to her father? I do not care how upset he was; he should have left the sex part out. Bitch-ass nigga! Aries ran toward the door, opened it while he was waiting for a cab outside, spit in his face, then slammed the door! Fuck that. She was tired and over his shit! She was not a fool and knew there was someone else in the picture. How the fuck he found an apartment that fast fuck out of here!

Although she knew the relationship was not going anywhere, she still wanted to try again and make things work. She still held on a little longer than she should have, but it was time-consuming. She was beginning to feel depressed, lost a lot of weight, lost her appetite, and smoked her lungs out until she did not have the strength to hold the blunt anymore. Her pillowcases were drenched in tears. Before she went out, Aries cried; and when she returned home, she cried some more. She called him throughout the day constantly. Sometimes she blocked her number and he would not pick up, and other times she unblocked it and he would not answer. When he did answer, she overheard his friends laughing.

It had been long overdue, and Aries still has not heard from Jason. She reached out to him again, and he finally answered.

"So you are never going to speak to me again?" Aries asked.

"I found someone else, and she treats me better than you," Jason said with sarcasm.

"She cooks for me, and she loves me," Jason went on.

"Oh please, I used to cook for you all the time and did a whole lot for you. When you were in a dark place, I left my homegirls to keep you company," Aries explained.

"You are just in your feelings. You barely know this girl, and she already loves you. Yeah, aight." Aries laughed.

"She does love me," Jason mentioned again.

"I bet your relationship will not last," Aries said.

"Whatever," Jason replied.

"I got to go," Jason ended the conversation.

After a while, she no longer recognized herself in the mirror anymore. She was broken and did not know how to get out of that brokenness until one day, she came across a flier on Facebook about an upcoming tour hosted by Tony Gaskin.

Upon her arrival, she saw Tony taking pictures and, of course, wasted no time taking a picture with him. While she was slowly walking away, she felt Tony's heavy hand on her shoulder. It was intense and obvious that the Holy Spirit was there. Aries did not dare to look back. Her eyes were watery, and she did not want him to see her in that light. Overall, she hated when she cried in front of others. She saw it as a sign of weakness. As soon as Aries got home, she could not help but pray and ask God for help and to detach herself from Jason. She even met with Bishop Curt Courtenay for additional help since she could not manage on her own. Special shout-outs to Tony Gaskin and Bishop Curt Courtenay! I love you both! Thank you for all your help.

Chapter 5

Blood

Ladies, never assume a man who is in a relationship will leave his girl to be with you. It does not matter how good you are in bed or how much you do for him. Once you hook up with a guy in a relationship, respect is out the window. Be ready to accept however he treats you.

It was Aries's cousin Jimmy from out of town. His girl, Denise, a.k.a. baby mother, and some dark-skinned dude parked in front of Aries's house, waiting for her to come out. The moment she saw the dark-skinned guy, Aries could not wait to find out who he was. Jimmy wasted no time introducing the two, and they all smoked a blunt before they pulled off to head to Denise's crib. Prior to that, Aries met Denise at Jimmy's house in the South. Aries needed somewhere to clear her head after her brother's passing and a break from Race. The South was not her permanent destination since she needed a vehicle to get around. Everything was so far. For instance, walking to a gas station was like walking seventy miles. It was nothing like New York. Besides, Aries liked noise; she never liked living somewhere too quiet. She always liked a combination of both. She loved her relatives and appreciated them even more during a time to escape from reality, but overall, the South was not a good fit for her. So when she met Denise and found out she was an Aries and from Brooklyn, she knew they would hit it off right away. Although Denise was much older than Aries, it did not stop them from developing a friendship. Also, if it was not for Jimmy and Denise, Aries would have been bored as fuck. They kept her entertained, and she needed that at the time.

Aries attended high school in the South but kept on being sent to detention, which was fun, by the way. The food was amazing, and the teacher was funny as hell with his strong Southern accent. Sometimes Aries and her late cousin would act out on purpose just so they could go to detention, and when they saw each other, it was nothing but love and laughter. Another thing Aries liked about detention was the infamous chicken sandwich. That sandwich was everything dead ass. If it were not for the cameras, she would have stuffed them in her backpack. During detention, no one was allowed to speak; and if you had to use the restroom, you had to raise your hand. Each student sat between cubicles and wrote a hundred times the reason they were in detention. It was the only way out or you stayed in longer. The teacher was always dressed in cowboy attire with his cowboy shoes; the only thing he was missing was a horse.

Education in the South was more complex than in New York. Aries not saying education in New York was not hard, but she had a better chance of succeeding there than in the South. There were more resources and staff to assist students individually whereas in the South, it was limited. It was more like a crash course for each course, and Aries was not a fast learner. Aries was more hands-on and a visual learner. Overall, she could not keep up with the curriculum. She even signed up for tutoring, hoping it would make a difference, but it did not. Her head was not in the right space at all, and all she thought about was her late brother. She cannot deny the fact that she receives a lot of love from her peers and the people who live in the neighborhood. Once they knew she was from New York and got comfortable, they addressed her as New York, and the rest was history.

Months later, Aries eventually returned to New York after going back and forth to the South. She missed home and her freedom. Of course, she will miss her relatives and new friends who are now family. But nothing can outdo New York. New York was her home for life and where she needed to be. Upon her return, Aries's parents moved into a new house, which was a five- to ten-minute ride from her former house. The house and her room, too, were way bigger than the last. Evidently, the room selected for Aries was her late brother's room, and she could not help to break down in silence. She could only imagine if he was alive, he would hook the shit out of this room. After studying her brother's room, Aries walked into the next room and knew it was not a good fit and took her brother's room instead.

In the beginning, it was cool living in the house until reality started to kick in, which was for Aries to get her life together for her late brother and herself. Back then, she thought she had all the time in the world and that having fun was a priority. As she got older, life went by much quicker than she anticipated, and that shit was scary and uncontrollable. Remember, time wastes on no one, so handle your business while you are young and have stamina. You will pay eventually in the long run, and it will become much harder as you get older. Do not think that because you are young, you can live however you want. Do not assume that your parents will always be around or take care of you. Life is short, and we all have to die. Have a mind of your own. Do not follow the crowd or waste time with people who are not helping you elevate in life. Those are not your real friends; those are seasonal friends.

Eventually, Aries picked herself up with the help of God and was inspired by her late brother's ambition, which is something she will forever cherish. Aries ended up graduating from high school and attending a two-year college. The days she did not have classes were the days she hung out with Denise most of the time. Besides, Denise's children were her cousins anyway. Here we go with the bullshit Aries said to herself. Denise gave Aries the heads-up about her dark-skinned friend who happened to be Monk. Monk was a goon, a troublemaker, very popular in his hood, and had a girlfriend. Aries was not surprised he had a girl because he was dark-skinned, good-looking, tall, and had full juicy big lips, which she wanted to suck and bite on. Monk did not fear no one and was well respected in the hood, so Aries knew she would be well protected. Aries respected Denise for looking out, but she wanted to learn more about Monk for herself. When someone warns you about something, believe and listen because the person actually cares for you; someone who does not care about you will not warn you at all.

Denise's apartment was the hangout spot. It did not matter what time you pulled up. As long as you had good energy, weed, and alcohol, then you were invited. Even though she was living with her mother at the time, it did not make a difference. Denise's mother was cool and loved by many. She was referred to as the mother on the block.

Ms. Robert was God-fearing and never afraid to spread the gospel to others. She was a great listener and always offered advice. But do not get it twisted; she will check you respectfully faster than a heart attack if you take her kindness for weakness. The only thing she complained about was smoking inside her apartment. She did not like the smell of weed.

Every time Aries visited Denise, she did not want to leave, and Denise had no problems with her spending the night too. Later down the line, as their friendship progressed, Aries considered Denise a big sister she never had. They were too alike. It was scary sometimes, especially when they got into a disagreement.

Aries was sitting on the couch when Denise checked the peephole to see who was at the door. It was Monk's fine ass. Denise reintroduced them. "Yeah, I remember her," he said while looking at Aries. "That is the kid's cousin." He sat right beside Aries, and they did not say much and just passed the blunts to each other. Unfortunately, Monk did not stay too long. Before he walked out the door, he slid a small piece of paper with his name and number to Aries and handed it to her, then looked back and winked at her. Aries thought it was cute for a goon like him to be old-school and smiled.

They spoke almost every day and had a strong chemistry. Talking to Monk was easy, and they share a lot in common. He was definitely aggressive and loud as fuck, but Aries did not mind. Monk wasted no time requesting to see her again, and she wasted no time wanting to see him too. The more they saw each other, the more emotions were involved. His girlfriend was pretty. Aries could not deny that. She wondered if she had any clue who she was. She wondered if she knew that Aries was about to fuck the hell out of her man and possibly steal him from her.

Damn, shit, OMG, touchdown! The sex was amazing, and he came with the full package. I mean bigger than an Amazon delivery van. I mean bigger than anything she could think of that was big.

My god! Monk knew exactly what he was doing, and Aries always came back for seconds. It went from visiting Denise to visiting Monk often. Of course, Denise felt a way because the attention was no longer on her. Aries tried to play it off sometimes and reassured Denise that she was not going anywhere, that they would always be cool; however, Denise was not buying that and knew what time it was.

Aries liked Monk so much that she wanted to have his baby. At one point, she thought she was pregnant. Her period did not come on time, and she was craving food like crazy. When she shared the news with Monk, he was happy and bragged to his friends about him becoming a father soon. They were the happiest and had big plans to raise the baby together and get married. A week later, Aries got her period, and she was pissed.

Good looks and a good dick comes with a lot of bullshit! It went from Monk and Aries spending time with each other every day down to one or two days out of the week. Yes, it is possible that on the days they did not see each other, he probably was with his girl, which was understandable. Aries knew what she signed up for from the start anyway. But when it is multiple bitches, then it is a problem. Aries was furious and could not believe this dude was so comfortable bringing another bitch around without her consent. It was not supposed to end up like this. She let his girlfriend slide because she was in the picture first. Now, he thought he was the shit. Aries did not care if they stopped speaking momentarily; he had no right bringing another chick around.

After a night of fun with Denise and her other friends at the club, Aries ended up spending the night. The next morning, someone knocked on the door. Denise opened the door.

"Yo, Monk wants to speak to you," Denise said.

"Nah. Tell him that I do not want to speak to him." And Aries returned to sleep. She was over his shit and did not want to have nothing to do with him. Afterward, Denise returned to the room to check on Aries to see how she was doing.

"What did he say?" Aries asked.

"He said he was sorry and begged to speak to you," Denise replied.

At that point, Aries lost interest in Monk. She was not going to lie. The feelings were still present, but she could not trust him or take him seriously. If he really want to take things seriously with Aries, he had to let go of every chick he was fucking, including his girl. That dick was too good, and she was not compromising for nothing.

Chapter 6

Ghost

When a man tells you he is not ready to settle down with anyone, though he has in the past, never assume something is wrong with you or something is wrong with him. In life, sometimes you meet a person at the wrong time. Timing is everything, believe it or not.

Never force a man to be with you after he tells you he is not looking for a relationship. It does not matter if you are attractive or kind; it will not make him change his mind. You can be the best thing that has happened to him, and he still will not give in. Now, if you continue to stick around whatever happens, then that is on you. You cannot get upset or feel some type of way because he let you know from the start that he is not looking for anything serious. Sticking around will hurt you longer. So if you like being hurt, by all means, stay. Do not beat yourself up, and be gentle with yourself whenever you have been rejected. It is okay and there are plenty of fish in the sea. Instead, use all the time you need while you are single to get your shit together. So when God sends the right man around, you will be able to recognize it, receive it, and embrace it.

It is rare when Aries comes across a guy who is honest from the start. Usually, when she meets a dude for the first time, it does not begin with the truth. Nowadays, some guys play too many games and are liars. So honesty goes a long way, and it turns her on. Yes, the truth could hurt at times, but she rather the truth than a lie. Aries respects any man who is upfront and lets her know what to expect rather than finding out on her own.

Do not get her wrong, not all men are after pussy. There are a few decent men out there who are willing and ready to settle down, but they all appear to be in movies for some reason.

On her way to church and walking toward her car, Aries ran into one of her neighbors who hollered at her frequently every time they ran into each other. It was clear she was not interested and used the same line that she was in a relationship to make him stop. Yes, the thirst was real. Sometimes consulting with God was not necessary due to the signs already there when certain guys tried to talk to her, especially Mase's ass. Mase was cool and someone she can smoke and talk to only. She never saw them two being a match; he was not her type. The moment she turned her head, she noticed this light-skinned tall brother sitting outside his steps. Light-skinned guys were definitely not on her to-do list, but she did not mind giving him a pass he was a dime piece. Mase noticed Aries checking him out, and she quickly played it off by staring inside her vehicle while listening to Mase's rant.

Prior to running into the light-skinned guy, Mase and Aries were having a conversation about warming up her car during the summer. He told her it was not necessary and that she could drive her car; nothing bad would happen to it. Meanwhile, she disagreed and believed it was needed.

"Only during the summer months you do not have to warm up your car. You can drive, nothing bad will happen to it," Mase said.

"Yo, bro, does a car have to be warmed up when it is hot outside?" Mase asked out loud to the light-skinned guy.

"Nah, it does not," the light-skinned dude replied.

"Thank you." Mase laughed.

Both men laugh at Aries. Aries proceeded to let her car warm up; she did not care what any of them had to say. It was her car, and she could do whatever she wanted with it.

At that point, Aries did not care about the topic and was mesmerized by the light-skinned guy's features. While Aries was getting ready to leave, Mase asked to be dropped off down the block. She did not mind and purposely kept on waving bye to the light-skinned dude before driving off. At first, he just looked at her and did not wave back, but she was not backing down, and eventually he waved back.

On her way back from her interview, she saw the light-skinned dude sitting outside on his steps, smoking a cigarette, and she intentionally parked her car right in front of his house. She thought to herself that this parking spot was reserved for her. Aries was excited and a little nervous at the same time. It was something about this guy that made her tremble in a good way. The brother was fine and better-looking than most of the guys she fucked with in the past. She just hoped he did not have any assumptions about her and Mase. It was now or never.

"Do you sell weed or know someone who does?" Aries asked.

"How much do you want to cop?" the light-skinned man asked.

"Forty," Aries responded.

"Okay," the light-skinned guy said.

The light-skinned dude got up and told Aries that he would be right back. Upon his return, they both waited for the bud man to arrive.

"You might as well make yourself comfortable. It is going to take a while for him to get here," the light-skinned guy mentioned.

"What is your name?" Aries asked.

"Red."

"Mine is Aries."

"How old are you?" Aries inquired.

"Twenty-three," Red replied.

"Damn you do not look your age. You look much older," Aries added.

Out of nowhere, Red started talking about his life; he was definitely an open book. Aries admired people like that in general because they did not care about what other people thought and you did not have to put too much effort into getting them to speak.

Red was tall, muscular, tatted up like crazy, and had nice coolie hair. She could not wait to run her fingers through his hair when it went down. His lips—do not get her started on the lips. It was pink, full, and looked like a delicious meal; and she could not wait to take a bite out of them. His eyes—he had the most adorable round puppy eyes that made her say "aww." His butt—it was firm and intact; she could not wait to rest her head on it. This man was a dime piece, something she was not used to seeing regularly. Usually, the guys who are unattractive are the ones who are always hitting on Aries, especially when she is outside, walking or minding her business or stuck in traffic. For instance, she could have the worst outfit, her hair not done, her teeth not brushed; and men would find a way to hit on her. Sometimes she liked the attention just a little bit, especially if she was not in the mood, and other times she ignored them.

The bud man finally pulled up and greeted them. She gave Red the money without making it hot. Red and the bud man went between the corridor doors and exchanged a few words, and he told Aries bye. Red handed the bud to Aries, and she smiled. That bud was smelling too good for her to not roll up one right away, but instead, she decided to wait until she got home.

They continued to speak a little longer than he told her he has to bust a couple of moves. When he got up, he passed his phone to Aries and aimed for a hug, then Aries took a step back and shook his hand instead. It definitely caught him by surprise based on his reaction. Without a doubt, Aries wanted to hug him, too, and squeeze the hell out of his dick. But she had to play cool and not appear thirsty.

As soon as Aries got in, she hurried to wash her hands, then took the oxtails out of the refrigerator that was seasoned the day before, and placed them on the stove. Next, she washed another pot and filled it up with water, added salt, and let it boil before adding the rice. Then she took out another pot, washed it, filled it up with a little bit of black pepper, and added salt and vegetables. Afterward, she went upstairs to change into something comfortable and returned downstairs to the living room. She then turned on the television and checked her phone periodically to see if Red texted her. From time to time, she would check her food to make sure it was not burning and tasted good. Out of all the beef in the world, oxtail takes the longest to cook. While Aries was watching something, she heard her ringer go off. She grabbed the phone to see who it was, and it was Red's fine ass confirming he got her number and was going to save it.

A few days went by, and Aries texted Red, asking what he was doing. There was no way she was going to avoid this brother; she wanted him, and she wanted him now! One night, Aries and Red were chilling in her car talking, drinking, and smoking; and she could not take her eyes off of him. The man was drop-dead gorgeous, and it would be a crime if she did not sleep with him. It may not be this exact night, but it will definitely be a night to remember. While Red was talking to Aries, she quickly interrupted him to acknowledge his honesty and the connection they had thus far. She wanted to show him how much she appreciated him by surprising him with a gift.

"I hate surprises. What is it?" Red asked.

"That is the point of it being a surprise. I promise you will like this surprise," Aries replied enthusiastically.

"Trust me, close your eyes," Aries went on.

When he finally opened up his eyes, he was in shock, blushing and smiling all around. His round puppy eyes were filled with so much joy and gratitude. Red reached for a kiss and thanked Aries repeatedly. At that point, she knew it was too early to fall in love, but she could not deny it. He was something special.

It was something about Red that stood out from the previous guys. Aries truly enjoyed his company and was so grateful that she did not have to travel far to see him. Whenever she was at work or school, she thought about him a lot, and her mind ran like crazy wondering how he was in bed. She could not help herself at times the man was fine. They did not speak much over the phone, but when they hung out, it was magical, and she never wanted it to conclude. She really felt like he was her soul mate. He was different. They had so much in common from their upbringing and spirituality to fake friends, fighting, and other traits.

A man who strokes hard back and forth does not mean he knows how to have sex. All you are doing is causing the woman's vagina to hurt and possibly have complications during birth. When having sex with a woman, you have to be gentle with the pussy, not beat it up like she stole something from you or she is your enemy. If you are that upset about something, do not take out your anger and frustration on the vagina. A woman's vagina is sensitive; use it with caution, please. There is nothing wrong with being a little aggressive in the bedroom but not to the point where the woman is more in pain than enjoying it. There is a big difference. Aries should not have to feel like she has to see a doctor right after she has had sex. Now, if the dick is worth it, she does not mind seeing a doctor. May God bless all men with big dicks and know how to use them. May you all live a long life. Amen.

In this case, God blessed him with a huge dick for no reason. How did he have a big dick and could not even use it? Each time they had sex, it felt like Aries was being run over by a four-wheel truck or taking her last breath. Sex is supposed to feel good, pleasurable, meaningful, and worthwhile and not feel like a horror movie. She was scared for her life. It was the type of pain where she needed to see a doctor to ensure her vagina could function the same. Aries did not understand how he could be this handsome and not know how to have sex. Even when he fingered her, it hurt. It felt like he was pinching her pussy rather than playing with it. The only good thing about his lips was that the brother knew how to kiss. He definitely did a horrible job eating her out. Instead of eating her out, he was chewing her out. She did not know if he was a monster. Not only that he sweated a lot. Goddamn! Aries knew she was too much in the bedroom, but c'mon, it was not fair his sweat kept on dripping down on her. She felt disgusted. At that point, she was turned the fuck off and wanted to throw a blanket over his body and walk out. It was too much. She would have been better off fucking someone else.

Even though Red sucked in bed, he still carried a special place in Aries's heart. She still wanted to take things to the next level by making things official but wanted to fuck someone else to make up for what he lacked. Yes, overall the sex was trash! She knew there was a good chance he would say no to being in a relationship with her, but she did not care to ask anyway.

It went from them fucking to Red going ghost on Aries for extensive periods of time. She did not understand why he did not have the decency to call or even shoot her a text. He would just take off and go about his business. No calls, no texts, and no response. The phone would just ring until it reached voice mail. The only time he did respond to her texts was when she wrote an essay cursing his ass out and telling him about himself, but whenever she wrote something positive, he ignored her. That shit annoyed the hell out of Aries because he was not the only one who did this to her, and she could not comprehend why people did shit like that. Some people are just fucking weird! She realizes when negativity is promoted, it has an effect on people instantly, whereas positively does not have that same effect. It should never have to go to that extreme real shit. Some people are just toxic.

When she finally saw him, they did not say a word to each other. Aries was really pissed about him ghosting her like she was nothing—a piece of trash. Even with them being friends, she deserved to know what was up with him. A friendship is not one-sided; both parties play a role in a friendship. It was fucked up on his end. When it came to the homies, he made himself available. When it came to his job, he made himself available. When it came to fighting and rescuing everyone else, he made himself available. So there was no excuse or justification for treating Aries like that. And when she finds herself doing more in a friendship or any relationship in general, she will take a step back.

"It is not only you that worries about me. My family does too," Red said.

"So you ghost your relatives too?" Aries exclaimed.

"Yes. I shut down on everyone," Red explained.

"Do you think it is right? God forbid something bad happens to you. How would anyone be able to reach you or help you if you are in trouble?" Aries asked.

"That makes no sense," Aries added.

"You have to do better because one day God forbid, it will backfire on you," Aries elaborated.

"You cannot be that selfish," Aries further explained.

"Yeah, I know," Red replied.

She was not buying his story and wanted to know the truth. Aries thought to herself that there had to be at least one person who knew his whereabouts. There was no way he could go away and no one knew where he was.

After multiple efforts and seeing their friendship one-sided, she decided to move forward and leave him behind. Aries was tired of playing along with his games and deserved so much more than what she was getting from him even if they were not an actual couple. They were still friends, and she could no longer continue to put in all the effort to make the friendship work if he kept ghosting her. So why should she give a fuck?

Chapter 7

Cop Caller

A man who lies often will suck the energy out of you and have you questioning your sanity.

A man with a hidden agenda is a dangerous man to date or trust.

A man who plays the victim lies a lot.

When you communicate with God and ask for his approval about someone you like or want to date, he says no. Listen to God, wait on God, or move on to the next. Whatever you do, consult with God first; and if you still do your own thing after God says no, you will suffer the consequences severely later on. Do not question God or become angry because he said no. There is a valid reason why he said no. Do not become curious and make irrational decisions after God said no; by then, it will be too late. Then your next prayer will be "Please, God, remove this person out of my life. Fix it, God!" But he told you no from the beginning. You should have listened.

God knows the man that you should spend the rest of your life with; he will not lead you astray, so trust God and pray often. He has good intentions for you, and he will not deceive you like the way people do.

Trust no one but God. People pretend very well.

Take your time when getting to know the man you want to date and his family. Getting to know someone is an ongoing process; it is not an overnight thing.

Do not rush into a relationship, and just focus on the physical part. A relationship is more than that.

"Once a cheater, always a cheater" only applies to fuckboys—and guys who want to be in polyamorous relationships.

When he says he loves you and does not hesitate to disrespect you, he really does not love you.

When he is not afraid to lose you, he really does not love you.

When he calls the cops on you, he hates you.

Never blame yourself for a toxic man's behavior; that is his problem, not yours! His ass was already toxic before you even came into the picture. You are good, sis.

Learn to distinguish the difference between a man who genuinely likes having you around versus a man who keeps you around because it is beneficial or uses you as his trophy.

A man will tell you he loves you and still treat you like shit.

You will know if a man loves you by the way he treats you, not what he says to you or how he looks at you.

Stay away from men who turn every conversation into an argument. Men as such are fucking toxic; you do not need that shit in your life. Life is already fucking hard as it is.

If he cannot treat you the way you should be treated, leave his ass immediately. Do not wait and stick around, hoping he will change for you.

He will never change if he is not willing to change.

You can be the best thing that has ever happened to a man who is not ready to receive you, and that is okay. Keep it pushing, sis.

There is nothing wrong with you. Do not blame yourself for how he mistreats you. Remember, misery likes company.

You cannot change a man no matter how much potential you see in him.

When people warn you about a man you are interested in, please take it into consideration and listen. One day, you will look back and thank them.

When you see red flags in the beginning, take them seriously, and do not throw them under the rug. Those red flags will save you from a lot of trouble ahead of time.

Do not allow loneliness to make you tolerate disrespect from a man.

Do not allow loneliness to make you settle just for any man.

Do not allow loneliness to make your mind wander or play mind games with you.

What you allow from a man is what you shall receive. So do not feel some sort of way when he treats you like shit, cheats on you, and lies to you. You remember you choose to stay.

Learning how to heal and love yourself takes time, so take all the time as needed fuck what anyone else thinks. It is your fucking life!

Do not jump into a new relationship as soon as you get out of a bad one. Heal first.

Stay single for a while until you are entirely ready to date again. Who cares if everyone around you is in a relationship? That is their chapter, not yours. Worry about you for once.

On a foggy night, Aries got off the 2 train and walked out of the subway station to her car. Out of nowhere, she looked back and saw a guy walking a few inches behind her, and he asked Aries if she did her own hair. At the time, Aries had no intentions of a new romance and wanted to try and concentrate on her well-being without any male drama. Aries told the guy no, she only did her own hair sometimes. She even wondered how in the hell did he notice her in the dark. Damn, this motherfucker got twenty-twenty vision. Aries could barely hear when someone called her out in the street. Literally, you have to shout or approach her. Even though she was mad at Red, he still had a special place in her heart. She knew it would be difficult meeting people who had no filter as he did. That shit was rare to find. In today's generation, people are quick to believe a lie over the truth. People will befriend a snake faster than someone who is real and genuine. People are distracted by social media; they worry more about what others think than what they see themselves as. All for likes, hearts, and followers rather than following God. This generation is sad. This generation is lost.

It kills Aries on the inside when she and Red were not on good terms, and it is obvious he feels the same too. Each time they ran into one another, both of their eyes locked. Anyone can tell they still had feelings for each other.

It was hard for her to pretend she did not care, but it was also hard for her to continue blowing up his phone. She got tired of being the first to contact him. She was not the one who initially exchanged numbers.

Aries needed a distraction to keep her mind from thinking about Red. It hurt her a lot that their friendship has reached its course, but now she was like "Fuck it! It is what it is." If he is not willing to make any effort to keep her around, then why should she? People make time for who they want without any excuses. The ones who make excuses are the ones who just do not want to fuck with you anymore and rather make excuses than tell you the truth. No one in this world is "that busy." It does not matter who you are.

She thought to herself how she will ever find "the one" if she does not put herself out there and try then stress over what did not work out. Honestly, she did not like the idea of starting over again, but she damn sure was not going to be single forever. Aries just wanted to be with someone and skip the getting-to-know-each-other part. That shit was time-consuming, and some men lie too damn much. She does not have time for that nonsense.

The fact that she has experienced so much disappointment and still desires to pursue love amazes her sometimes. By now she would have given up on love and got a puppy instead, yet she chose love still. Just so we are clear, there is absolutely nothing wrong with having both. She did not want to leave this earth without fulfilling all her goals. She wanted to leave a legacy behind for her family and her children. Deep down, she always knew she was meant to do great things in this world even though she had no clue what her purpose was. She knew that God created her to do big things and after the loss of her brother and many more thereafter. She had to take her life seriously.

Aries told the guy she did her hair sometimes but not other people's hair.

"It looks nice," the guy said.

"Thank you," Aries replied.

"You are welcome," the man responded.

"What is your name?" he asked.

"Aries."

"You?" Aries asked.

"Leon."

"How old are you?" Aries asked.

"Thirty-eight," Leon responded.

"Damn, you do not look your age," Aries said surprisingly.

"What about you?" Leon asked.

"Thirty-two," Aries replied.

Aries still did not believe his age, so he pulled out his ID. Aries was surprised.

He laughed.

"You do not look thirty-two. More like fifteen," Leon went on saying.

She was flattered and was used to people telling her she looked much younger than her real age. She likes that shit and saw it as a blessing to be old and look young as fuck. Thank you, God, and thanks to my parents!

As soon as Aries saw her car, she was ready to get in and drive off, but the conversation made her stay just a little longer. She told herself the moment she noticed a drop of rain she was out. Leon ask Aries if she smokes. She had a blank stare to his question. As much as she wanted to after having a long day at work, traveling between trains late at night, she kindly declined. She did not know Leon well enough to just smoke with him. He could be a criminal for all she knows.

"What is your sign?" Aries inquired.

"Taurus," Leon mentioned with a smirk on his face.

The moment she heard his response, she threw up the peace sign and told him she was out. He told her, "Wait, wait, do not leave." He's one of the good ones and would not hurt her. She did not fall for what he was saying but liked what she was hearing at the time. Remember, she was still trying to get over Red's fine ass although he played himself. Besides, it had been a while since she heard a man say something nice to her.

"When is your birthday?" Aries asked.

"April 24." Leon responded. Aries did not know much about April Tauruses men; and only knew about May Tauruses men. She purposely brought up Race and Red and used them as an example since they both broke her heart, and she did not want her heart to be broken again. He reassured her that she had nothing to worry about and that he was a good, loving man who could be trusted. Leon explained.

He sure had Aries's mind running that night. She felt like she was dreaming for once, talking to a man who was not after her pussy and having meaningful conversations with her. He asked Aries for her number. Aries asked him if he had Facebook and took down his details. He wished her a good night and told her to reach out to him. While Aries was waiting for her car to warm up, it started to rain, and she noticed Leon walking to a building but was not too sure if it was the right one or not. He definitely looked puzzled. For a quick second, she thought about offering him a ride to get to the right destination and then changed her mind and made a left turn at the stop sign to head home. He appeared smart, and she was certain he would find his way, or maybe he was mesmerized by her looks, and she giggled before busting the turn.

It took Aries a few weeks to hit up Leon on Facebook, and he did not respond to her DM right away. It seemed like he did not remember her at all, but then again, she was not surprised. It had been a while since they last saw each other.

She shot him a DM, asking if he remembered her or not. When he finally read the messages, he wasted no time sending her a friend request. Next thing you know, her phone was vibrating like crazy. At first, it creeped her out. He liked throwback pictures and current ones. He definitely utilized the like button a lot and even commented underneath some of her pictures and statuses. Aries just hoped he was not a stalker that was all. He gave Aries his number, and from that point on, the rest was history.

The first time they spoke on the phone, Leon was living in Upstate New York. It threw Aries off guard a little. What if they happen to get serious one day? She did not want to date someone long-distance shit; she could not even handle dating a guy locally. What makes you think she will handle a long-distance relationship? Hell no! He told her he was living with his mother temporarily to help her out with his nephews since it was taking a toll on his mother's health. Aries thought it was helpful of him to put in the time and effort to help out his sister and his mother. In the beginning, Aries did not analyze the situation thoroughly but eventually had concerns. What happened to his sister? What happened to the kid's father? Why were the children in the care of their grandmother?

One day, Aries was on the phone with Leon, and she heard a commotion in the background between him and a woman's voice. All she heard was shouting and cursing between the two, and the profanity was mainly coming from him. The louder it got, the more irritated Aries got; and after a while, she could not keep quiet.

"Who was that?" Aries asked.

"My mother," Leon replied.

Oh wow, she could not believe it was his mother. She would have never imagined that, and from the sound of things, it was not the first dispute between the two. It was the kind of curse words you say to a random person, not your mother—the type of argument that would grab people's attention to record and share all over social media, the type of argument if a police officer was nearby, one would immediately intervene. It definitely caught Aries by surprise, and she did not know if she should hang up the phone right away or remain talking to him like it never happened. The crazy part about this was they both had something in common: Neither of them got along with one of their parents. For Aries, it was her father. So if they ever became serious, they would be able to relate to and understand one another. As nice as that sounded, it did not quite end up that way, but keep reading, though.

Thereafter, they spent a lot of time talking on the phone frequently. The way he thought and analyzed shit this nigga was smart as fuck. He was not the type of guy Aries would normally like, but she did gravity to his mind immediately. He was different, not the average guy. Prior to that, her conversations always begin with "Hey, what are you doing? I miss you. I want to see you." No guy ever took the time to feed her mind the way Leon did. Some men were only focused on getting a nut but not taken her seriously. Although she was not into politics, the shape of the earth, Islam, and topics that would put her to sleep, Aries still had a listening ear. Overall, she liked learning and being exposed to new things.

They spent hours talking on the phone every day. He planned to meet up with her after work.

The moment he saw her, he ran toward Aries and lifted her up. It was refreshing. Aries had not been lifted like that in a while. She is not going to even lie; it did make her blush a little, and she was just as happy but in a calmer way. Her instinct kept on reminding her about the last relationship that went sour, but her heart was telling her just give him a chance you never know. Aries was scared. She was so used to getting hurt that she stopped believing in love after a while.

Although Aries was not pleased with Leon cursing the shit out of his mother, she was not perfect herself either, so who was she to judge him?

He was sweet, funny, spoiled the hell out of her, supportive, and always made her feel special. She liked the idea of having him around and being herself. He treated her with so much admiration that sometimes it was overwhelming to process. Aries was not used to that, and she did not know how to respond to it. She wanted to move at a slower pace, but he came at full speed, and she was not prepared. It just felt surreal. It felt like a movie scene or better yet her dreaming. She could not believe this was actually happening to her.

She tried to do anything to keep her mind off of Red; she was really hurting and mad at the fact that he did not care. So since he did not care and was still ghosting her, it was time for her to see what Leon had to offer rather than spending time talking to him on the phone. She was eager to connect with him on a spiritual level and see how he conducted himself in church.

Brooklyn Tabernacle in downtown Brooklyn was not her church home but a church that hosted Christmas eve services annually for the public free of charge. Aries was shocked he enjoyed the service, but she did not like when Leon was being disruptive during the sermon. He would murmur things whenever he disagreed with what the pastor said. She understood as clearly as day that people are entitled to their opinion, which is cool; however, there is a time and place for everything, and downplaying or discrediting the pastor for preaching the Word is not cool, nor does it make yourself look cool—that shit is whack as hell. Show some respect. Each time he did it, Aries told him to stop and save it for another time.

The night was young and cold. Aries was ready to head back home; however, Leon was not ready to leave and offered to take her out to eat. During that time, she did not have any cash and proceeded to head home, but he insisted on taking her out. As they sat and waited for their drinks and food to come out, Aries noticed one of the side chicks Race was dealing with. She did not want to make a scene and leave a bad impression, but her skin was boiling. All she could think about was Race and what the hell he saw in this girl. She gained a lot of weight and was far from pretty, but as she got closer, she realized the girl was pregnant, and it made sense why she put on so much weight. Aries could not help to alert Leon about the girl. Besides, she would always care about Race no matter who she was, seeing that man was still her everything.

In the middle of their conversation, the drinks came out. Aries noticed Leon had more cherries than she did. Halfway through his cup, she asked him if he wanted the cherries since they were just sitting there, waiting to be devoured. He shouted at her. *What the hell was that about?* she thought to herself. It left a distaste in her mouth, and she was ready to conclude the date. She did not understand how it even reached that point. All she did was ask him a question, and he got upset for no reason. Aries was pissed and tried her best to not let the tears come out by looking in the opposite direction. When he noticed her body language, he removed the cherry from his cup and put it in her cup and apologized for shouting at her. Of course, she ate it but she was still mad. Since there was a lot of tension in the room, they decided to leave.

While sitting in the train station, the part of Leon yelling at Aries kept on replaying in her mind, which meant she was really angry. She was curious to know what was that about and put him in his place to never yell at her again, but at the same time, she did not want to talk about it in public. Aries decided she would wait to talk about it over the phone or forget it even happened and move forward. Leon was nice enough to ride with Aries throughout the train ride until she got off her stop and walked to her car. She did not even bother to offer him a ride but thanked him for the night spent together. He told her to text or call him when she reached home.

Immediately, Leon contacted Aries to find out if she made it home, and they spoke for hours; he even invited her for a Christmas feast at his aunt's house. (As the mask begins to unravel down the line, Aries eventually finds out they are not related by blood. Leon was just close with her family.) Aries was thrilled and nervous at the same time. When she meets a guy's family for the first time, all she could think about was being interrogated. Nothing good ever comes out of that. While they were sitting in Aries's car, waiting for it to warm up, they engaged in a brief conversation, and out of nowhere this motherfucker raised his voice at her again. She did not say anything at the time because when she looked up, she saw Red crossing the street, and she did not want to draw attention, so she let it slide again but she was pissed.

Surprisingly, Leon's aunt was so sweet and welcoming to Aries. The woman could throw down in the kitchen. Do not get me started on the drinks from eggnogs to other alcoholic beverages; it was fucking amazing! Thank God the environment was chill and no interrogation! Nevertheless, the only thing that threw Aries off was Leon wanting to leave the dinner table to smoke. Mind you, they smoked throughout the car ride, so she did not understand why he could not just wait until it was time to leave. Damn, he was feening. He even asked Aries to step outside with him. At first, she hesitated because she did not want to be judged by his family; but at the same token, she did not know his family well enough to be left alone with them.

Toward the end of this lovely dinner, the aunt ended it by praying for Aries. It definitely caught her off guard and meant something to Aries. She was curious to know why she prayed for her, though. She wondered if that prayer was a sign from God or if the aunt was warning Aries about Leon. Whatever the reason, she really appreciated it, and it was definitely the highlight of the night.

The next time they spoke, Aries invited Leon to accompany her to Atlantic City, which was already paid for prior to the invitation. That was one thing Aries liked to do was travel alone or with people; it all depended on the mood she was in. He agreed to go with her and use her car to drive out there. Mind you, around this time, she was back the fuck up and needed some dick ASAP.

At first, she was playing hard to get to see his reaction; but when they finally kissed, she wanted to see what else he was good at, and he had no problem sliding his average dick slowly from the back. When he ate her out, he took her soul out at the same time. The man knew what he was doing, and Aries held his head down a little longer. Shit, he got that hurricane tongue too! They fucked so much that she was not interested in participating in any of the amenities at the hotel; she just wanted to smoke some blunts and continue fucking him. Taking a break was not an option unless they were sleeping, and they started their sessions all over again. She was unstoppable, a beast in the bedroom. He was a miracle and had her cumming nonstop. At times, Leon even pleaded with Aries to get out of the room and check out the hotel amenities or eat, which she eventually did. Even though they went out, she could not help to think about how good the dick was and wanted more. There was no way in hell she was going to leave Atlantic City without getting dessert—the best dessert she had in a really long time! The sex was bananas! And she could not resist it. He was so good that she forgot how Red looked.

Back to reality! The worst part of vacation was returning home. She hated it here. She was still on cloud nine and could not wait to ride the hell out of Leon. He was a skillful man who took care of his masterpiece in bed. She had no complaints about his performance; he definitely exceeded her expectations. Damn, where the hell had he been hiding all this time? She could have been fucking him a long time ago, she thought to herself and laughed.

Leon not only met Aries's expectations in the bedroom but other expectations, too, like spending quality time and being affectionate with her. From the outside looking in, it looked like they lived together because he was always around. There were times she would beg him to not come over so she could focus on her studies, and he promised her he would not distract her. Aries could not help but say yes it was hard to turn him away, especially when he brought weed and munchies and gave good head. In addition, they had pillows fights. It was fun having him around while it lasted. Keep reading.

Being around Leon was organic; he was different, and Aries liked that.

"What are you doing for New Year's?" Aries asked.

"My aunt is having a party," Leon replied.

"You should come," Leon inquired.

"Okay," Aries said.

Aries would only come to the party under one condition: he would go to church with her first.

The moment she came downstairs, he gave her a lot of compliments and asked her if she had anything to eat since he was hungry. She asked him why he did not eat before he came to see her, and he told her he was rushing to get to her to avoid being late. Fortunately, her grandfather had dropped off Haitian patties to her mother earlier, and Aries retrieved two out of the box and gave him one and kept the other for herself. She wanted to see if he would like it first before handing him another one. Besides, she did not like seeing food go to waste, especially food that tasted good. Just as fast as she gave him the patty was just as fast as he ate it. Yeah, he definitely was hungry!

"Why was there not enough meat in the dough?" Leon asked.

"Maybe the person who made it did not add enough meat or have enough meat," Aries explained.

"Everyone makes patties different," Aries elaborated.

"Do you like it?" Aries asked.

"Yes," Leon said.

"Do you want more?" Aries asked.

"Yes," Leon responded.

Aries thought to herself, *Hopefully, the patties with something to drink would fill him up until church was over.*

She was hesitant about introducing one of her favorites in the world—Bishop, her father figure—to Leon. She had a feeling he would not like him or feared Bishop would shake his hand after service and tell Aries a revelation of some sort. She was a little bothered that this fool slept throughout the service; but if they were at a party, concert, or watching Netflix, his ass would be wide awake. They took pictures after service, and Aries chilled with her homegirl for a few and they left. She ended up dropping her homegirl home, and they spoke in Creole throughout the ride.

On their way back to Aries's house, Leon asked her if she had fifty cents. She did but told him no and asked why. He wanted to stop by the store and get something to eat. She told him it was not necessary since there were plenty of patties left. Plus, they were about to go out anyway; all she needed to do was change her clothes. This asshole decided to shout at Aries while in the car. Mind you, it was after 1:00 a.m. People were still sleeping, and he just did not care. Aries turned her head to the right and noticed a police car and told Leon to lower his voice or he was going to draw attention. He got even louder. At this point, she was fed up and told his ass to pull over. So he pulled over aggressively, got out of the car, and continued to disrespect her and threw a bag of shoes on the ground and stomp both of his feet like a fucking toddler. It was disgusting and an embarrassing view. She can understand a toddler behaving in that manner, but for a thirtysomething-year-old man, it was unacceptable. Aries reminded herself that it was a new year and to not get out of character just reflect on today's sermon and go inside the house. Since he was acting a fool, she did not want to risk going inside right of way and stood behind the tree in front of her steps and observed his next move. She did not trust him and she damn sure was not going to let him damage her car.

She knew he was hungry, but how was a fifty-cent snack going to fill his ass up? If anything, that shit would make him hungrier. She was embarrassed and pissed. Lord knows how many of her noisy neighbors got up and looked through their windows or stood behind their doors, watching and listening to Leon act a damn fool.

This nigga done lost his mind. He was so loud that he ended up waking up Aries's dad. The moment she walked in, he was coming down the stairs, and she explained what happened. He said he heard a man's voice yelling but had no idea the man was yelling at her. The entire time, he thought it was random people just arguing. It made her feel more like shit to hear her father say that. She was furious, confused, and just wanted to be alone. All she could think about was rolling a blunt, eating, and going right to sleep. Instead, she went on Facebook to post a picture of her outfit like she always did every new year. She then checked her message, and it was Leon, who posted a video crying and apologizing. At first, she thought it was a cute gesture to admit he was wrong, but she did not have the guts to forgive right away. This was not the first time and probably would not be the last.

A few weeks after his tantrum, they made up and everything was back to normal. Leon was still spending time with Aries consistently and showing her lots of attention. She enjoyed every moment of it and did not want things to conclude. Aries thought about taking another trip with him, and this time it would be to Las Vegas. Leon was excited; he had a childhood friend who resided there whom he has not seen in ages. Aries did not mind him catching up with his friend as long as he did not make the entire stay about his friend. In addition, Leon suggested for Aries and him to get the same hairstyle since they both had dreadlocks and also color-coordinate their outfits, which was something they often did.

Aries was surprised to hear when Leon told her it was his first time taking the plane. This whole time, she thought he traveled by air before. It just confirmed that she did good by inviting him on this trip. After hours of sitting on the plane, she was highly annoyed, hungry, and sleepy. From the looks of things, she did not have the energy to eat and just wanted to rest. Leon's friend ended up lost and could not find us at the airport. Aries assumed that him living in Las Vegas was a lie; maybe he was visiting someone. It took him a good hour and a half to finally notice us standing outside.

She wasted no time studying this dude and instantly smelled trouble. Aries can see why Leon was eager to tag along. All she knew was he better keep his trouble-looking self elsewhere because she was not with the shits and damn sure was not going to be disappointed during this trip either. The whole point of this getaway was to celebrate passing all her classes with or without Leon. His friend also appeared to be mentally unstable. Aries made sure to keep a close eye on him.

Leon was so happy to see Tommy. After checking in, Leon told Aries to order food and hand over the money while he headed outside to attend to his friend. Aries immediately asked him where he was going, and he responded, "Outside."

Aries said, "Outside to talk or outside to go out?" She needed clarity. He told her to go out, then she said, "What is the point of ordering food if you are going to be out with Tommy?"

"Why can you not wait until the next day to see him?" Aries exclaimed.

She also reminded him that the point of the trip was for them to have fun alone, not spend the entire vacation with Tommy. He made Aries irritated even more, like who does that? Your girl is tired, hungry as fuck, and eventually want to settle in bed with her man. Instead, he wanted to run off with his friend. That shit was whack, and Aries was not going to let it slide neither.

While eating her food and watching television, Aries heard a knock on the door, and she opened it and saw Leon. From the looks of things, it was going to be a long daunting trip. If she knew his plans was to chill with his boy more than her, she would have never invited him to begin with.

No offense to the LGBT community, but she really was beginning to think Leon was into men big-time. It was always difficult to turn down his male friends, and sometimes he would purposely start an argument just so Aries could leave while he goes and hangs out with his boys. Does it not sound suspicious to you? Help me out here. I know I am not overreacting. She never dated a guy who gets more excited hanging out with his homeboys than his girlfriend. It was uncomfortable. She understood they have not seen each other in a while, but that is not an excuse to carry on like that.

Anything she wanted to do, he was not interested in listening. It had to be his plans and his way, or he would ruin the entire trip, which he eventually did. He then proceeded to start an argument and call everybody in their mother and spread lies about Aries. Bitch-ass, lying-ass cornball! The people who believe his lies probably did not know him very well or knew his temperament and enabled his behavior anyway. When you enable or ignore someone's temper and erratic behavior, you are just as wrong as that person. A real one is going to tell you the truth and will call you out on your bullshit when you are acting a fool. So Aries was highly annoyed that this individual he called was feeding into the lies he shared. It was a damn shame. This motherfucker was an open book but not in a good way. He would start shit, lie, then play the victim. She was not the type of chick to involve people that have nothing to do with them in their relationship. Whatever issues they had stayed with them. Involving other people in your relationship will only add fuel to the problem. They are not there when he disrespects and humiliates her in public or behind closed doors.

His idea of fun was smoking weed, chilling with Tommy, and walking on the strip. No guy in his right mind is going to walk on the strip just to catch a breath of fresh air and catch up. No, it was more than that. This is Vegas, henny. Hennything is possible. All Aries wanted to do was hit up a few clubs, go out to eat, participate in fun activities and, of course, walk on the strip last. When they finally got to the club, Aries specifically warned Leon that he cannot smoke weed inside the club but could smoke outside. Next thing you know, he started smoking weed and passed it to Aries. She declined. After the first pull, all Aries saw were two men approaching them and escorting Leon out of the club while Aries just stood there, disappointed. For the most part, she was surprised this nigga even cooperated 'cause he always want to pick a fight with others since he swear he was unstoppable and hardcore. She wasted a whole outfit and got cute for nothing. All she could think about was how he did this shit intentionally just so he could be around Tommy's ass. After that happened, he still wanted to go out, but Aries was over it and wanted to return to the hotel.

She could no longer take Leon's reckless mouth, especially on a trip he did not contribute to. Even if he did, it still does not make it right to be mistreated. Aries wasted no time calling security to escort this manic out of her room. She wasted no time canceling his return flight and switching hotel rooms since he had an extra key. Of course, Aries was not surprised when he attempted to justify his actions and debate with security about why he should leave, but thank God the security staff remained professional and did not entertain his bullshit. He likes to challenge others and get a reaction out of them. That was one of the many of his traits. He loves to be the center of attention and wants to be in control of everything. If you are someone who does not partake in the drama, he will become more aggressive and more hostile until he has the final say. Thank God again, the security staff did not stoop to his level and maintain their professionalism. Besides, they outnumbered his ass anyway. There was no way he could take all of them down alone. They would have tased his ass and kept that big mouth shut. There was no way Aries was going to put up with Leon's erratic behaviors; he needed to leave with his ungrateful ass!

Upon her return from Vegas, Aries had not heard from Leon to her surprise. Normally, when they were not speaking, he called her a lot or even popped up at her house. Being the caring person that she was, she ended up calling him to make sure he got back to New York safe. It has been three weeks since they have not spoken.

"Did you make it home?" Aries asked.

"Why do you want to know?" Leon replied.

"You do not fucking care! You left me," Leon shouted.

"You left me stranded in Vegas, and I had to call so many people to book my ticket in order to return home," Leon shouted.

Aries told him she was not calling to argue, she just wanted to know if he made it home safe. He started going off about Aries not being a good girlfriend and how evil she was and claimed his aunt and his friends were right about her although they knew nothing about Aries. Just so you know, this was not the same aunt who prayed for her. After his rants, he then hung up the phone."

Since their last conversation, he was acting more distant and Aries heard less of him. Every time she called him, either he answered the phone shouting or put her on "Do Not Disturb," and that was when she began questioning everything. She had a feeling he was creeping around. Like any typical fuckboy, he denied the truth and used working long hours or being restless as an excuse. He really thought Aries was a fool and failed to realize that it was so convenient for him to bring other girls around since he was taking care of an elderly man he lived with at the time.

After months without speaking, Aries decided to give Leon a ring and asked him to come over to set up her iPhone." While speaking to him, she sensed the tone in his voice. He sounded really angry about something. Aries did not know where all this anger came from, and she damn sure did not want to be around that energy. She knew how it would end. He agreed to come over.

As soon as he walked in, Aries could smell the tension in the room, and she wondered if he was still upset about being left behind in Vegas. Laughing my ass off! Whatever it was, she regret inviting him over.

She passed Leon her iPhone, and he grabbed the remote to turn on the television. At first, he was flicking through the channels. Then here he went with the bullshit, watching YouTube about conspiracy theories, Islam, COVID-19, Trump, and any bullshit that she did not like to watch. By the way, most of their arguments always led to Leon forcing Aries to watch YouTube videos and then he would elaborate about the videos. Hence, when she did not pay him any mind, he would get upset, argue, and be ready to kick her out of the apartment that one of his bitches fucking gave to him freely. Whereas if she was watching something, he criticized her about it. Selfish prick!

Did this nigga just throw her brand-new iPhone on the ground, knowing the phone was fragile? Oh hell naw! At this point, Aries saw red and took something from him and threw it on the ground too! Yup, two wrongs do not make it right, but in this case, it was right for her. Enough is enough! He does not know how to use his inside voice and got the nerve to damage Aries's property. He then got up and aimed to hit Aries after they both were wrestling. He eventually got ahold of the door to get out of her bedroom, and she ran after him. Fuck you going, nigga! She was not done just yet. She remembered all the disrespect she tolerated and had enough. Aries had it with him and ran to the kitchen to retrieve a knife that she was not going to use; she just did that to scare him away. The look on his face gave him away too. This was not the first time he was used to this shit with his toxic ass! She ran directly toward him with the knife pointing it to his chest, then paused and thought about the repercussions of her actions if she stabbed him. He was not worth going to jail. He eventually got out of the house, ran to his car, and sat there, pretending to be in pain while holding on to his chest.

Did this asshole just call the police, playing the victim and pretending he was injured while holding on to his chest? What an actor, and the award goes to Leon the most conniving snake of the year! This nigga was wicked! Aries did not even stab him. The knife never went through his chest. If that were the case, his ass would be dead today. Wow, Aries was speechless.

From that point on, nothing would ever be the same anymore. Aries could never look at Leon the same anymore. Whatever feelings she had left for him were buried six feet deep. He went from "playing the nice guy" to now an enemy for life! No one in history has ever violated her as he did. She was nervous, confused, scared, and did not know what to do. She has never been arrested, never had any prior record, never broken the law or even stepped foot into a precinct. And he knew that and still fucking called the police. She did not know if she should remain inside or run outside to speak to the cops so they could hear her side of the story—the truth—rather than listen to his lies.

Aries's father advised her to not run outside with the knife. Now, she really wanted to stab him for real. Her mind was running and it drove her crazy. She decided to do the right thing as she assumed and told the police her version of the story—the truth. If she knew prior, the truth would have put her in handcuffs. She would have never run outside in the first place. She would have acted like Leon beat the shit out of her so he got arrested instead of her.

He made her believe he was different and genuine in the beginning, then turned around and got her arrested. You do not do this act to someone you claim you love. She was not the one who said she loved him first. She never loved him. He did. Bitch-ass nigga. Who calls the cop on his girl over a fucking disagreement, which was part of a fucking relationship?

Her first arrest, her first offense, her first time walking into a precinct, her first time being fingerprinted, her first mug shot, her first court appearance, and her first time in front of a judge. Her first time feeling like a criminal, and her first time feeling like her freedom was stripped away. Aries could not believe how fast the paramedics came to rescue his ass as if he was seriously injured. All she did was poke his ass with a knife, and it did not go through his skin. No blood or nothing came out. All gloves were off. Aries hated this nigga! He really did not love her as he said he did. This whole time he was her secret enemy—the devil agent.

Leon knows the law so well and how it works, whereas Aries does not know anything about the law, and he uses that to his advantage. Instead of being a real man and educating her about the law, he broke her into pieces and made her feel like shit. So many questions ran through her mind. She could not breathe and was dying to go home so she could return to work the following day and put all this behind her. As easy as that may sound, it did not happen that way.

While Aries was sitting in a cold ass cell, waiting to hear from a detective or be seen by anyone, a tall white man with glasses walked toward her cell and asked Aries how long she was dating Leon. Then he shared an overview of Leon's criminal rap sheet. Aries could not believe this whole time that she was dating a criminal. This motherfucker could have killed her. She informed the detective that she was not dating him around the time he committed those crimes, and the detective walked away.

Aries was thankful the detective disclosed that vital information to her. It was fucked up that Leon had a dark past without even mentioning it to her. God forbid something bad could have happened to her. She did not know who he has problems with or if he is affiliated with any gangs. She wondered what else he was lying about.

Fast forward, Aries was able to get a lawyer who was recommended and paid for by her father and released thereafter. Thank God she did not have to see a judge or go to court due to COVID-19. The case was dismissed, and Aries was happy to return to work, but her mind was still running; she was traumatized even when she was out. Now, she fears being around any cops and does not trust them.

She hated Leon and will never forgive him for this. The fact that he did not hesitate or think twice about calling the cops confirms how he really felt about her. You do not do that to someone you claim you love, only someone you hate. With everything that is going on in this world today, police brutality targets black men and women the most, and this is what he does. What if the officers had killed Aries or sexually assaulted her? He did not consider any of those factors.

One day, boredom struck, and Aries decided to pop up at Leon's job. Before heading to ring the doorbell, Aries observed his favorite drink and a spliff in a silver car. *Who could this be?* Aries thought to herself. So she decided to do the unthinkable and sat in her car for hours, waiting for them to come out. As soon as the door opened, Aries saw a chick, and then she got out of her car and walked in her direction. While walking, Leon came out and turned his head to the left and was in shock to see Aries. It was like he saw a ghost. He also mumbled something under his breath. What confused the hell out of Aries was the simple fact that Leon refused to call it quits with her but did not have a problem fucking other bitches. Like be with them other bitches and leave her the fuck alone. She knew it would never be the same again after he got her arrested. So she did not care that he was fucking other bitches; she already knew it would happen after Vegas. He uses his penis to cope with his issues but fails to realize having sex with multiple women will only give him and the girls an STD. He thinks chasing bitches is a fucking accomplishment at his age. Like, nigga, you are almost dead. Her plan was not to fight the chick, but she definitely got some answers without a doubt. The fact that this nigga was comfortable cheating on a block with a bunch of noisy neighbors and cameras everywhere was mind-blowing. No wonder some of the neighbors looked at him in a disgusting manner and felt sorry for Aries. This motherfucker was heartless, selfish, and just did not give a fuck and it hurt Aries a lot. This was a workplace, and he turned it into a trap house. No regard whatsoever for the elderly man he was taking care of and robbed behind his back. He would use his chase card like it was his to buy weed, clothes and spend the money on bitches rather than pay his debt or car insurance. With that brain of his, he could have used the money to start his own business or give back to the community. Then when he runs out of money, he goes around begging people for money. So fucking pitiful.

Luckily, this girl was not rude or on some fighting shit and told Aries everything. Aries could not believe this shit was happening right under her nose. The fact that he constantly lied to her and made her think she was the only one in the picture. By all means, Aries was not a fool. She had a strong feeling he was fooling around. She noticed after Vegas "the nice guy act was over."

This nigga played the shit out of both of them and every girl he was involved with. He did not even care about his actions. He only pretended to act like he was sorry because he got caught the fourth time by Aries. When God blocks you from being with a guy, it is not because he does not want to see you happy or he hates you. He intervenes because he knows this person is not good for you. Look at God's blocking as your protection because he truly cares for you and does not want to see you suffer with a guy who does not sincerely mean right by you. At first, Aries could not understand why God was doing this to her. The more he got caught by Aries, the more the arguments continued. He was so comfortable fooling around with multiple chicks. Even when they were not together, he was still hiding it from her.

Aries and his bitch knocked on the door since his pussy ass wanted to remain inside. That was another thing Aries disliked about him. He's quick to do wrong to others, and when he gets caught, he either plays dumb or pretends to be sorry. Aries recorded his ass admitting to saying he loved the girl after she questioned him. All Aries saw was red and proceeded to kick his ass, and he closed the door while she banged on it. As soon as she turned her back, she heard the police sirens, ran off, got in her car, and drove. "Bitch-ass nigga," she said to herself.

She was furious but not surprised at Leon. She still could not grasp the fact that he did not want to leave her alone no matter how many times he cheated on her. His ass was very selfish. Aries knew she was better off without him.

Each year, Aries renews her security license as a backup plan just in case things do not work out for her when seeking employment. For some odd reason, it took longer than expected for it to arrive in the mail. Normally, it takes about three weeks maximum, but this time months went by, and something was off. She contacted the license renewal department of state to inquire about the status of her security license and was told by one customer representative who knew how to provide the correct information besides the other representatives who had no clue what they were talking about. Shit was annoying because she had to go through different prompts and put on hold for a long-ass time before speaking to anyone. Sometimes she did not speak to anyone. So this honest representative advised her that her application was on hold and someone from the office would reach out to her. That was all she could say. Aries was nervous and confused as hell. Meanwhile, she still wanted to pursue getting a restraining order against Leon. She had enough of his bullshit and no longer wanted to be in his life anymore. She knew this dead-end relationship was not going anywhere, and all it was doing was delaying her blessings and causing more destruction in her life.

The officer came out with a police report for Aries to fill out and ask her for her ID. While filling out the form, the officer came out with sadness on his face and informed Aries that she had an I-9 card. During that time, Aries had no clue what an I-9 card was and asked the officer to elaborate. Unfortunately, the officer told Aries that she would have to go to another precinct to get more details. Right then and there, it all made perfect sense why her security license was on hold. When she got home, she went on Facebook and read her messages, and you will not believe what she read. Leon had the audacity to tell her the elderly man called the police on her. She knew he was lying. That man would never get involved in Leon's drama unless Leon threatened to harm him, which made more sense since he was afraid of Leon. He had too much to lose and said the detectives would be knocking on her door real soon. Leon must have thought by giving Aries the heads-up, he was doing a good deed. Fuck that. He knew exactly what he was doing and did not give a fuck! Heartless son of a bitch! Aries hated him! This nigga calls the cops for everything.

Aries could not believe this was happening all over again. When is this nigga ever going to take accountability for his actions? When is he ever going to tell the truth for once and stop blaming his wrongdoings on others? When is he going to stop purposely hurting her like this? It is like he gets an adrenaline rush every time he calls the police. He brought all this chaos to himself and thinks he could get away with it by calling the fucking police instead of taking responsibility, being honest, and communicating like an adult. It was not like she begged him to be with her. They were not dating at the time; she only was fucking and smoking his weed, and he was aware of it. However, for some reason, every time they had sex, in his mind they were a couple.

While the detectives were banging on her door, Aries was getting dressed to go to her photoshoot to promote her clothing store. There was no way she was going to let Leon's bum ass stop her from fulfilling her dreams. As hard as it was, she had to keep pushing until she saw results. Once it was clear and those dickheads left, she hopped in a Lyft to attend her photo shoot. Her mind was running, and she could not stop thinking about this idiot who called the cops on her for the second time. She was extremely upset and more stupid for going back to him.

The good thing about this experience for Aries was that God never left her side. He was always there even when the people were against her in the courtroom and portrayed her to be a criminal over a man who fed them lies and has a serious mental illness, a man who is unhappy with himself, a man who fucked multiple women and smoked his lungs out all day and night to numb his pain, a man who has mommy and daddy issues and channeled his anger out on others, a man who possessed narcissistic characteristics. God already knew the demons Leon had, and there was no way he was going to allow Leon to make Aries lose herself and everything she worked so hard for. Leon may know the criminal justice system better than her, but Aries knows God better than him and has a relationship with him. She also believes in karma and believes his karma is coming if it had not come already.

Chapter 8

Where Are They Now?

Race ("Lovebug")

The last time Aries heard from Race was when she was living in Georgia. He apologized for all the pain he cost her and reminisced about every moment they spent together. He even told her she was his best friend. Aries accepted his apology and missed the hell out of him despite the things he put her through. The love that she has for him will never fade away. He told her he has a daughter and issues with his child's mother. Currently, he resides in Philadelphia.

After their last conversation, Aries wanted to stay in touch with Race, but his phone number was no longer in service. She even reached out to his friends on social media, and no one has heard from him. She hoped he was okay.

Rasheed ("The Married Man")

Rasheed did not give up on Aries. His ass still wanted to fuck her even though he had a wife. Their intimacy lasted for a while on and off before she blocked him and he moved out of state. She was in her feelings that he left, but she knew it was for the best. She will always have love for him no matter what, and as long as they can remain cordial without sex, then their friendship will last forever. Neither of them was going anywhere.

Jahiem ("The Ideal Boyfriend")

Wow, Jahiem grew up and became a man, finally! Aries assumed he did his bid in prison, and it definitely changed him for the better. She was very proud of him. He now has his travel consulting business and is an author and a mentor based on what she saw on his Facebook page. What really caught her by surprise and made her heart almost stop beating was when she saw the word "Engaged" as his relationship status. So she decided to put on her investigator lens and do some digging. Damn, this bitch was ugly, and she had a kid.

At first, she thought he was lying when he told her over the phone months before that he was seeing someone serious and wanted to extend an invitation to Aries but feared she would wild the fuck out. Aries kept on asking him an invitation for what? A wedding or a baby shower? He did not want to tell her and immediately changed the topic.

Now looking back, she understood what the invitation was for. Wow! She was shocked. It was a slap to my face—the ultimate betrayal. That bitch did not deserve him, only she did. Why did he choose to become a man now? Why was he not a man when they were together? It was not fair how she invested her life with this man for him to end up with someone else who already has a child. Now, he is going to be a stepfather and soon become a husband and possibly have more kids with this bitch. Aries was upset and even shed a tear. She should have been the one to be his fiancée, not this bitch. Aries definitely felt some way this one really hits home. She does not hate him, but she could never speak to him again.

Jason ("Womanizer")

What the fuck is wrong with her? Aries must have been the experimental girlfriend all along. First, Jahiem, and now Jason. She never thought in a million years that Jason, the cheater, the womanizer, the player, would settle down with anyone. Shit, that applies to Jahiem too.

To make matters worse, no offense to the LGBT community, his new girl looks like a straight dude. Yo, she dead-ass looks like him. That is crazy! She questioned herself and wondered why they were not acting right when she was in the picture. They decide to grow up and make another woman happy other than her. Yes, she is in her feelings. It is not fair! She was beginning to think she does not have a happy ending like everyone else. The bitch is mad ugly and looks like a transgender man into a woman. Better yet, if Jason was a woman, that is how he would look. They look like twins. Aries could not stop laughing. She even called Laura to give her the update, and she was laughing as well. He had no problem showing her off all over social media, which he never did with Aries.

Prior to that, if she saw Jason in any public setting, she would be so quick to curse him out or throw something at him. Thanks to Bishop, if she runs into him today, she would look him dead in the eye and keep it pushing. That animosity she once had toward him has subdued.

Thank you, God and Bishop, for giving me the strength and deliverance to move forward and never look back.

Monk ("Blood")

Monk is something else. He and Aries had spoken a few times over the phone and even made plans to see each other since he lived in another state now. At first, Aries considered giving him a chance until one time, they were speaking, and he was shouting and talking shit about a girl he was living with while she was in the background. Aries could not believe he was doing that and being disrespectful in someone else's house, not paying any rent, not working, and only prescribing her dick. Wow. Some people just refuse to change and do better. Some people rather remain comfortable and stagnant. Aries was not feeling Monk at all, and thank God she did not fall into his trap again. She took everything she went through with Leon to avoid going through that with Monk. They were not far apart from each other and acted out in the same manner. Aries had no problem being only friends with him, but he did not agree to it and was blocked afterward. She deserved way better than Monk; he was not it, and it does not matter the history that they had.

Red ("Ghost")

Aries has not heard from or seen Red since the last time they spoke. She really believes his entire family has moved to another neighborhood during COVID-19. Normally, she would run into him or his father and sometimes his siblings. Now, she does not see any of them, and it has been like this for some months now. Lately, when she goes outside, she always sees his friends without him. She even thought about asking one of his best friends about his whereabouts but did not want to appear desperate since Red has her number and knows where to find her.

It is what it is, but she really misses him and could use a hug and a friend right about now. I love you, Red, always did and always have. I am so sorry for pushing you away and allowing my emotions to get the best of me. I am sorry for not being empathetic in the time of need and for allowing my emotions to win. I did not fully honor our friendship and made it about me. I am truly sorry and hope we can start over and become friends again. I love you. You were one of the realest individuals I ever crossed paths with, and I hope we can see each other again. I love you, Red. I know I will not get that again because nowadays, everyone is fake. Please find it in your heart to forgive me.

Leon ("Cop Caller")

Aries wished this nigga would die already. God is taking too long. She could not understand someone who has a reckless mouth, acts hardcore, puts fear in others, and has 911 on speed dial! Please give me a fucking break, you pussy! I hope you are reading this too. Do not say I did not warn you, Leon; you are going to cause your own death. He swears he can go around being disrespectful to anyone and not deal with the repercussions of his actions. Not everyone will tolerate such disrespect and have patience as Aries did. He is definitely going to pay one way or the other.

Leon will never learn or grow up no matter how old he is. He is going to continue chasing after pussy whether he is in a relationship or not, whether he is engaged or not, and whether he is married or not. He is never going to be faithful, and it is what it is. He will continue to be conniving and controlling. At this point, only God could perform a miracle and change him no one else can. Honestly, I do not even think God wants anything to do with him. He does not even respect God and uses his name in vain.

Aries hopes he dies! She is tired of him. No one in history has ever violated her and worn her out mentality as he did. Fuck you, Leon! Your karma is coming.

About the Author

I always dreamed of getting married one day and being the mother of five handsome boys. I guess God had other plans for me or my selection of men sucks! Whatever it is, my ass is still not in a relationship.

What's good? My name is Esther E. Laurenceau. I am the middle child of three and the only girl. I was born and raised in Kings County Hospital, also known as Killer County. I was the only one that gave my mother a C-section, and to this day, she complains about how much pain I cost her and will sometimes show me her scar. All I could say was damn, I had a big-ass head and weighed a lot!

Thank God, I grew up with both of my parents in one household, yet only one parent raised me. My mother is more of a sweetheart, and my father is an asshole.

I am a high school and college graduate. I went to Brooklyn Comprehensive Night High School. I attended one of the best schools Metropolitan College of New York from August 2016 to June 2019 and obtained my bachelor's degree in human services and was the first in my intermediate to earn that degree. Shout-outs to me! I was fortunate to be taught by high-league professionals who were compassionate and cared about the students. Since the age of fourteen, I have worked multiple jobs. My ultimate goal is to become an entrepreneur and be my own boss, make my own rules, and create a schedule that gives me the freedom to live life to the fullest. I do not want to spend my entire life being an employee working for someone else and making their dreams come true and adding more money into his/her pockets. I want to be in control and do what I want in a productive way while making money and living my life. You only get one life; there are no second chances in life, so why not make the best of it? I do not want to die old, bitter, and with regrets. I want to die old, looking young and at peace.